NAPOLEON HILL'S
POWER
OF POSITIVE ACTION

AN OFFICIAL PUBLICATION OF
THE NAPOLEON HILL FOUNDATION

TO CLAIM YOUR ADDITIONAL FREE RESOURCES, PLEASE VISIT SOUNDWISDOM.COM/NAPHILL

SOUND WISDOM

PO Box 310

Shippensburg, PA 17257-0310

For more information on publishing and distribution rights, call 717-530-2122 or info@soundwisdom.com. Reach us on the Internet: www.soundwisdom.com.

Quantity Sales. Special discounts are available on quantity purchases by corporations, associations, and others. For details, contact the Sales Department at Sound Wisdom by calling 717-530-2122 or emailing info@soundwisdom.com.

For international rights inquiries, please contact The Napoleon Hill Foundation at 276-328-6700 or email NapoleonHill@uvawise.edu.

Written by Napoleon Hill with contemporary commentary by Judith Williamson, Director, Napoleon Hill World Learning Center.

ISBN TP: 978-0-7684-1017-4

ISBN Ebook: 978-0-7684-1018-1

For Worldwide Distribution, Printed in the U.S.A.

Previous version published as ISBN: 978-1-937641-16-0.

DEDICATION

Dedicated to all the readers of and contributors to the weekly *Napoleon Hill Yesterday and Today* ezine.

CONTENTS

Foreword by *Judith Williamson* 7

Chapter 1   What You Think About You Bring About. 9

Chapter 2   Major Attributes of Personal Initiative. 13

Chapter 3   21-Day Challenge. 17

Chapter 4   Twelve Great Riches of Life. 22

Chapter 5   The Quest for Success .27

Chapter 6   Seventeen Success Principles. 30

Chapter 7   The Substance of Success 34

Chapter 8   Demolishing Barriers 38

Chapter 9   The End of the Rainbow 41

Chapter 10   Inch by Inch it's a Cinch 45

Chapter 11   Recognize the Value of Others. 49

Chapter 12   Fear Not. 53

Chapter 13   Cultivate Creative Vision 57

Chapter 14   Positive Attitude Attributes 62

Chapter 15   Accurate Thinkers. 65

Chapter 16   Launching Dreams. 69

Chapter 17   Values Determine Actions 73

Chapter 18   A Wealthy Mindset 76

Chapter 19   "What Do I Do Next?" (Fear of Poverty) 79

Chapter 20   Create a Better You (Fear of Criticism) 83

Chapter 21   Choose a Healthy Lifestyle (Fear of Ill Health). . .87

Chapter 22   Hope Replaces Emptiness (Fear of Loss of Love) . . .90

Chapter 23   Embrace Every Stage of Life (Fear of Old Age). . .93

Chapter 24 Book Worm Benefits (Fear of Losing Liberty)....96

Chapter 25 Remembering the Good Times (Fear of Death)..99

Chapter 26 Personality Power.......................103

Chapter 27 Opinions—Cheapest Commodity on Earth...106

Chapter 28 Define Problems 109

Chapter 29 Accept Assistance.......................112

Chapter 30 Positive Purpose........................115

Chapter 31 Improvement, not Perfection.............118

Chapter 32 Take Care of Yourself 123

Chapter 33 Faithful Versus Fearful 126

Chapter 34 The Energy of Emotion 129

Chapter 35 Life after Death........................133

Chapter 36 Freedom—An Earned Privilege............137

Chapter 37 Self-Sabotage 140

Chapter 38 Hate—A Robber Baron....................143

Chapter 39 Your Ultimate Purpose 146

Chapter 40 Demand Life's Best 149

Chapter 41 Expect Change..........................152

Chapter 42 Life's Drifters and Non-Drifters 155

Chapter 43 Choosing a Pacemaker....................159

Chapter 44 Positive Self-Talk 162

Chapter 45 Your "Other Self" 166

Chapter 46 Ten Commandments of Success 170

Chapter 47 The Value of a Sound Character 174

Chapter 48 Self-Confidence Formula.................177

Chapter 49 Your True Calling 182

Chapter 50 The Time has Come 186

FOREWORD

Napoleon Hill co-authored a successful book with W. Clement Stone, whose first commandment of success is "Do it now" and take advantage of the *Power of Positive Action!* Considering this viewpoint and popular command, those of us who follow this advice accomplish more, have less stress, live with fewer regrets, become more self-disciplined, and demonstrate personal persistence. All of these qualities contribute to making our unique world a better place in which to live simply by *doing it now.*

When you consider things that remain undone, there is seemingly a reverse process in the universe that causes these things to unravel and become knotted and unruly. Left to their own resources, these items on our forgotten to-do lists take on lives of their own. They lurk in crowded basements, overstuffed closets, fermenting refrigerators, and moldy clothes bins. If only they were addressed in a timely fashion, they would not be organizing an uprising and playing havoc in our lives. By doing it now, a person can avoid all this overcrowding and resistance that materializes in front of our very eyes.

When we take positive action before someone tells us that we have to do it, we exert our independence, strengthen our self-discipline muscle, negate our stress level, sharpen our persistence saw, and unite with the law of attraction. If we fail to act now, the very opposite outcomes appear and eventually wear us down. Good habits breed good outcomes, and an action becomes a habit over a period of repetition. This repetition ingrains the habit into our lifestyle, and sooner rather than later we become a model for this behavior. We become doers instead of procrastinators.

If you decide to take positive action now, you will begin to reap the benefits immediately. As you work through the following chapters, you decree to your subconscious mind that you are an action-oriented person who accepts no excuses. By doing, you kick in the reciprocal action of receiving since it is the cycle that naturally occurs. The strength of the action coupled with the determination to achieve the outcome is a powerful process that will not be overcome. By taking personal initiative with a positive mindset, you will decree your future one action at a time. Start now, don't delay your reward. Plug into the *Power of Positive Action* and qualify for the treasures in life that you deserve.

By reading a chapter a week and following through with action appropriate to the message, you will become known in a very short period of time in your local community for being a person who grabs the reins and advances forward.

If you do a little extra, you will be known nationally as a person who can be counted on to get the job done.

And finally, if you go the extra mile by doing just a little beyond what you did previously, you will be known in the international circuit as a person who is a doer and creator. By working through this process, you become the scriptwriter for your life's story and the creator of your own advancement and success.

You will sacrifice all the goodness life has to offer if you fail to use the *Power of Positive Action.*

Be your very best always.

—JUDY WILLIAMSON

Chapter 1

WHAT YOU THINK ABOUT, YOU BRING ABOUT

Those who have suffered a tragedy need to know that they are loved and cared about. They need to feel that they have not been forgotten and left to their own devices. Doing little things for such people does not entail much effort or time and generally little money, but it will mean all the difference to those to whom you show such kindness.

—Eliezer Alperstein

As mentioned in the Foreword, if you read one chapter a week from this book, you will notice that each month I include an explicit suggestion for maintaining a positive mental attitude combined with an expression of gratitude. One of my favorites is what I call the Napoleon Hill Gratitude Prayer. Simply, it states, "Oh, Lord, I ask not for more blessings, but for more wisdom with which to make better use of the blessings you gave me at birth—the privilege of controlling and directing my own mind to purposes of my choice."

Rather than asking for more money, more time, or more possessions, this prayer asks for more wisdom to appreciate and enjoy what we already have. If we reflect for a moment on this thought, we will begin to understand that there is abundance all around us and we need not seek out more when we haven't even used or come close to exhausting what we already possess. Things that money can't really buy such as a healthy family, meaningful employment, longevity, wisdom, and life-long friendships are things that we need to acknowledge and be thankful for in our daily lives.

By reciting this prayer frequently, we are notifying our sub-conscious mind that we already live in abundance, not lack. Since thoughts work like magnets and attract what we think about, these positive thoughts of gratitude will bring more of the same into our lives. Generally, we find what we are look-ing for, and when we put ourselves on notice as to the things we are grateful for in our lives, more come our way. *What you think about you bring about!*

Positive thoughts of gratitude, coupled with affirming prayer, bring about more of the preferred conditions in our lives. Dr. Hill's prayer is non-denominational, direct, and to the point. This prayer can provide us with guidance for improved living; but in order to profit from this guidance, we need to take action in the direction of our own choosing. As you learn to ask for direction from a source outside of yourself, miraculously the answers will be found where you never con-sidered looking—within the talents you were gifted at birth. These are your true treasures. Take them out of storage, dust them off, polish them up, and put them to use for the benefit of yourself and others.

Auto-Suggestion and the Law of Attraction

Dr. Napoleon Hill

There is a law, which we may properly call the law of attraction, through the operation of which water seeks its level, and everything throughout the universe of a like nature seeks its kind. If it were not for this law, which is as immutable as the law of gravitation which keeps the planets in their proper places, the cells out of which an oak tree grows might scamper away and become mixed with the cells out of which the poplar grows, thereby producing a tree that would be part poplar and part oak. But such a phenomenon has never been heard of.

Following this law of attraction a little further, we can see how it works out among men and women. We know that successful, prosperous people of affairs seek the companionship of their own kind, while the down-and-outers seek their kind, and this happens just as naturally as water flows downhill.

Like attracts like, a fact that is indisputable.

Then, if it is true that people are constantly seeking the companionship of those whose ideas and thoughts harmonize with their own, can you not see the importance of so controlling and directing your thoughts and ideals that you will eventually develop exactly the kind of "magnet" in your brain that you wish to serve as an attraction in drawing others to you?

If it is true that the very presence of any thought in your conscious mind has a tendency to arouse you to bodily activity that will correspond with the nature of the thought, can you not see the advantage of selecting, with care, the thoughts which you allow your mind to dwell upon?

Read these lines carefully, think over and digest the meaning they convey, because we are now laying the foundation for a scientific truth which constitutes the very foundation upon which all worthwhile human accomplishment is based. We are beginning, now, to build the roadway over which you will travel out of the wilderness of doubt, discouragement, uncertainty and failure, and we want you to familiarize yourself with every inch of this road.

No one knows what thought is, but every philosopher and every person of scientific ability who has given any study to the subject is in accord with the statement that thought is a powerful form of energy which directs the activities of the human body; that every idea held in the mind through prolonged, concentrated thought takes on permanent form and continues to affect the bodily activities according to its nature, either consciously or unconsciously.

Auto-suggestion, which is nothing more or less than an idea held in the mind, through thought, is the only known principle through which people may literally make themselves over, after any pattern they may choose.

Source: Adapted from Napoleon Hill's Magazine, July 1921; pages 22-23.

Chapter 2

MAJOR ATTRIBUTES OF PERSONAL INITIATIVE

The choice to read, study, and apply worthwhile reading material will help decide whether you are successful or just wonder what happened. Successful people need no alibis while unsuccessful people make excuses for their place in life. Make the choice to be a faithful reader and encourage those close to you to do the same.

—DON GREEN

Napoleon Hill would not head the list today of self-help authors unless he took personal initiative at critical points in his career. From accepting the challenge to complete a "philosophy of success" from Andrew Carnegie to accepting W. Clement Stone's challenge to come out of retirement to finish his life's work, Napoleon Hill rallied to the cause. In either case if he had failed to do so, his volumes of research would not appear on the shelves of countless successful businesspeople of the past, present, and yet to be born!

Carnegie and Stone serve as bookends to Dr. Hill's lifetime achievements. Each provided a motivational spark that

Hill fanned into a personal flame in order to literally fire up his personal commitment to a cause that he chose to dedicate his life to—and that cause is the Science of Success. This "science" uncovers the principles of personal achievement that any person can learn and master. However, two things must be in place: self-discipline and personal initiative.

In his research, Dr. Hill found that it required a synchronized system of success that included interacting principles. These principles address mental, social, physical, emotional, financial, and spiritual aspects of the holistic human being. Today, and for his time, this was innovative research and development at its best. Recent findings corroborate Dr. Hill's unique approach to viewing humankind from what I term the "Renaissance approach." Human beings are multifaceted, and for a system to work, each identifiable component must be addressed and engaged. Just as our bodies are groupings of interacting, functioning systems, so too is the Science of Success an interactive, living philosophy.

Yet today, Dr. Hill is the only writer on success who brings together a system for *individual* achievement. This system must be recognized, studied, and then applied for a person to reach his or her utmost potential. Like recipes found in a cookbook, a person must utilize many interconnecting skills in order to produce the spectacular gourmet meal in all its courses that others admire. Piecemeal, you may only have a salad or dessert, but having a purpose and a plan to attain it makes the results nutritious and tasty too. So it is with the Science of Success. Do not be content with only fluff. Go for the main course and you will be once and for all completely satisfied.

The Major Attributes of Personal Initiative

Dr. Napoleon Hill

Personal initiative heads the list of qualities a successful leader must possess. These qualities are:

- Personal initiative.

- The adoption of a definite major purpose.

- A motive to inspire continuous action in pursuit of a definite major purpose.

- A master mind alliance through which you may acquire the power to attain your definite purpose.

- Self-reliance in proportion to the scope and object of your major purpose.

- Self-discipline sufficient to insure mastery of the head and the heart, and to sustain your motives until they have been realized.

- Persistence, based on the will to win.

- A well-developed imagination, controlled and directed.

- The habit of reaching definite and prompt decisions.

- The habit of basing opinions on known facts instead of relying on guesswork.

- The habit of going the extra mile.

- The capacity to generate enthusiasm at will, and to control it.

- A well-developed sense of details.

- The capacity to take criticism without resentment.

- Familiarity with the ten basic motives that inspire all human action.

- The capacity to concentrate your full attention upon one task at a time.

- Willingness to accept full responsibility for the mistakes of subordinates.

- The habit of recognizing the merits and abilities of others.

- A positive mental attitude at all times.

- The habit of assuming full responsibility for any job or task undertaken.

- The capacity for applied faith.

- Patience with subordinates and associates.

- The habit of following through with any task once begun.

- The habit of emphasizing thoroughness instead of speed.

- Dependability, the only requirement of leadership that can be stated with one word—but no less important to success on that account.

There are qualities of minor importance which leadership in many fields of endeavor may require, but these listed are on the "must" list of all able leaders. Measure any successful leader by the list and observe how many of the traits that leader applies, although he or she may do so unconsciously.

Source: Adapted from *PMA: Science of Success,* Educational Edition, Napoleon Hill Foundation, 1983; pages 201-203.

Chapter 3

21-DAY CHALLENGE

I have not missed a day in years of doing my Morning Ritual of positive statements, and encourage my clients to do likewise. Because I'm convinced that I will default to the general negativity of our society if I start to slip, not unlike alcoholics who think they can have just one drink.

—JIM ROHRBACH

Are you addicted to self-defeating behaviors that spiral you downward into the depths of negativity or even depression? Why not take the 21-day challenge, and make the shift to a positive outlook and improved well-being? Here are some simple things that you can do to ready yourself for a more positive attitude in the days ahead:

INSTEAD OF THIS:	DO THIS:
PHYSICAL	
Eating junk food	Eat fruit and veggies
Being sedentary	Walk for 15 minutes every day
Over-sleeping	Awaken 30 minutes early and meditate

INSTEAD OF THIS:	DO THIS:
MENTAL	
Watching too much TV	Learn a skill
Being closed-minded	Consider another point of view
Scanning depressing news reports	Read a classic
EMOTIONAL	
Decreasing personal contact	Seek new acquaintances
Growing angry	Focus on peace
Preferring to be alone	Seek out community
SOCIAL	
Failing to communicate	Listen more
Declining social invitations	Host a get-together
Losing friendships	Acquire new acquaintances
FINANCIAL	
Spending money	Save money
Wasting funds	Invest funds
Losing control	Document control
SPIRITUAL	
Lacking gratitude	Notice gifts
Refusing to look deeper	Consider the Source of Life
Refraining from rituals	Try new approaches

You may notice that these suggestions are general in nature. You may also notice that they relate to the six aspects that many consider the components of who we are and how we define ourselves. This is done with a purpose, so that you can add the detail and reinforce the changes and modifications you need to specifically make in your own life. Why not print out the list and add the details as they apply to you? Try this prescription for a healthier, happier you for 21 days; then if you honestly replaced habits that spiral you downward with ones that can skyrocket you in life, write me and tell me about your success at nhf@purduecal.edu. Be the change for others to emulate!

The Major Attributes of Human Engineering in the Home

Dr. Napoleon Hill

Once upon a time not too long ago, a farmer, living in the mountainous section of one of the Southern states, brought home a new wife to become the stepmother of his two small boys. The wife brought with her two sons of her own, and in due time a fifth son was born of the marriage.

The home was typical of that mountain country, and the farmer was the product of four generations of his people born and reared in poverty and illiteracy.

His wife, however, came from a more prosperous section of the state and had received the benefits of a cultural background and a college education. She was not the type to accept poverty and illiteracy without protest.

The evening on which the farmer brought his new wife to their home, he introduced her to relatives and friends who had gathered there for the wedding reception. And finally he introduced her to his eldest son, a lad of nine years, with the following words:

"And now I wish you to meet the fellow who is distinguished for being the worst boy in this county and will probably start throwing rocks at you no later than tomorrow morning."

The stepmother went over to the young "Jessie James," placed her hand under his chin, tilted his head upward, looked him squarely in the eyes for a moment, and then turned to her husband and said, "You are wrong. This is not the worst boy in the county, but the smartest, who has not yet found the proper outlet for his enthusiasm."

Then and there began a friendship between that young boy and his new mother which was destined to project its influence for good throughout more than half of the civilized world. That was the first time anyone had ever called the boy smart. His relatives, including his father, as well as all the neighbors, had built him up in his own mind as being a bad boy, and he had not disappointed them. His stepmother, in one brief sentence, changed all that!

Think of this story, fathers and mothers, for you have it within your power to influence your youngsters. You may be inspired to work miracles in the lives of some who need only the right influence to give them a start on the road that leads to happiness.

The stepmother was a small woman, but what she lacked in size she more than made up in ambition and enthusiasm. The week after she came into that poverty-stricken home, she held a master mind meeting with her husband which was destined to force him to part forever with poverty. At the end of the meeting it was announced that he was to enroll in a dental college. The following year, at the age of thirty-eight, he matriculated at the Louisville Dental College in Kentucky, where he remained until he was graduated.

Source: *PMA: Science of Success,* Educational Edition, Napoleon Hill Foundation, 1983; pages 257-259.

Chapter 4

TWELVE GREAT RICHES OF LIFE

Failure isn't a genetically inherited condition. It is a "gift" which is often bestowed upon us with the birthday cakes our mothers bake and the hunting trips we take with our dads. It is a "present" wrapped with ribbons, bows and fancy wrapping paper we receive at our doorstep like a letter bomb sent with no return address.

—ELIEZER ALPERSTEIN

Poverty is a state of mind and it is also one of the seven basic fears. Feeling poor in spirit or in your financial status is first a thought that is followed by the corresponding emotion. Thinking and feeling poor only feeds the cycle of poverty. Think on the things that bring richness into your life. These things do not have to cost money, although they can. A good way to start the practice of rich thinking is to consider Napoleon Hill's Twelve Great Riches of Life and how you can bring these closer to your reality day by day.

1. A Positive Mental Attitude. Purposefully think pleasant thoughts and these thoughts will exhibit

"attraction power" that will draw good things into your life. For example, focus on finding that single perfect flower and when you do, buy it and display it on your table or desk for all to admire. Costs little, but pulls in positive vibrations.

2. Sound Physical Health. Eat well, exercise daily, and move your body hourly for optimum results.

3. Harmony in Human Relations. Talk less, listen more. Condition yourself to consider another's point of view.

4. Freedom from Fear. Exchange your fears for faith and refuse to worry about something that you cannot control.

5. The Hope of Future Achievement. Set simple goals and live up to your expectations. Start small and work up!

6. The Capacity for Faith. Read faith-based stories for inspiration, and seek out similar experiences in your own life.

7. Willingness to Share Your Blessings. Give from your current earnings, not only from your surplus.

8. A Labor of Love. Do something that you enjoy for the pure joy of doing it.

9. An Open Mind on All Subjects. Challenge yourself to grow and exceed the space you now occupy in the world. Go beyond where you are and learn something new.

10. Self-Discipline. Budget your time and money and create a daily plan for the maintenance of

sound health. A little done each day adds up in a month's time.

11. The Capacity to Understand People. School yourself in the nine basic motives that inspire people to do things. Next, consider your primary and secondary motives—good or bad. You are where you are in life because of the actions you take.

12. Economic Security. Plan for your financial security by saving a set portion of your weekly income. Never become someone's servant or slave due to lack of personal finances.

When you acquire a "nose" for these twelve riches of life, you will truly be a blessing to yourself and others and also a success by the best ruler for measuring a life well-lived. It's been said that success by the yard is hard, but by the inch it's a cinch.

The Mastery of Poverty

Dr. Napoleon Hill

Poverty is the result of a negative condition of the mind, which practically every living person experiences at one time or another. It is the first and the most disastrous of the seven basic fears, but it is only a state of mind, and like the other six fears, it is subject to the control of the individual.

The fact that a major portion of all people are born in surroundings of poverty, accept it as inescapable, and go with it all though their lives, indicates how potent a factor it is in the lives of people. It may well be that poverty is one of the testing devices with which the Creator separates the weak from the strong, for it is a notable fact that those who master poverty become rich not only in material things, but also rich and often wise in spiritual values as well.

I have observed that people who have mastered poverty invariably have a keen sense of Faith in their ability to master practically everything else which stands in the way of their progress; while those who have accepted poverty as inescapable show signs of weakness in many other directions. In no case have I known anyone who had accepted poverty as unavoidable, who had not failed also to exercise that great Gift of the power to take possession of their own mind-power (as the Creator intended all people should do).

All people go through testing periods throughout their lives, under many circumstances, which clearly disclose whether or not they have accepted and used the Great Gift of exclusive control over their own mind-power. And I have observed that along with this Great Gift from the Infinite go also definite penalties for neglect to embrace and use the Gift, and definite rewards for its recognition and use.

One of the more important rewards for its use consists in complete freedom from the entire seven basic fears and all the lesser fears, with full access to the magic power of FAITH to take the place of the fears.

The penalties for neglect to embrace and use this Great Gift are legion. In addition to all of the seven basic fears, there are many other liabilities not included with these fears. One of the major penalties for failure to use the Great Gift is the total impossibility of attaining peace of mind.

Source: Adapted from You Can Work Your Own Miracles by Napoleon Hill, Fawcett-Columbine, NY, 1971; pages 72-73.

Chapter 5

THE QUEST FOR SUCCESS

If at the age of 47, I can begin the transformation from being a Marine to being a physician, anyone is capable of transforming himself into something else as well. My grandfather popularized the saying, "What the mind can conceive and believe, it can achieve." Believe it.

—Dr. J. B. Hill

As we journey through life, our definition of success may change and become more comprehensive. Seldom do we desire the exact same things that we may have worked so hard to earn in our early years. As we work to define what is meaningful to us at every stage of our lives, it is good to have a standard to work from, and I feel Napoleon Hill's definition of success is as good as any. He defines success as our God-given right to have what we desire from life as long as we do not violate or infringe upon the rights of another living human being.

In taking this definition into account, it makes good sense because it establishes parameters for what we can and can't do. No lying, cheating, or stealing will be tolerated since those actions do infringe on another's rights. No dictatorial visions of grandeur either that place one or many persons under our control. No—nothing can be aspired to that reaches outward rather than inward because the true locus of control for our personal mission in life is centered inside each of us. We must look within to be fulfilled in our outer world. What literally makes us tick will be the mission in life that we are the most comfortable pursuing because that is what brings us joy. By doing what we love, we place ourselves in the "timeless" zone where our work also becomes our play, our mission then mirrors our passion in life.

No doubt about it, prospecting for our buried treasure takes work. Mining the gold inside each of us takes effort, skill, dedication, personal initiative, and eventually—if we are successful at it—all the Seventeen Principles of Success. That is why the admonition "Know thyself!" is such good advice as we seek to define what success really looks like for us.

A Message on Success

Dr. Napoleon Hill

Success is the most enchanting word in the English language.

Tell the average person that SUCCESS is the attainment of whatever one wants in life without interfering with the rights of anyone else and that the very first step to be taken in procuring it is development of the habit of rendering more service than paid for—and your words will fall on ears that hear but do not understand.

But, tell a person that SUCCESS means money and unless that person is one of the proverbial few who really understand how to succeed he or she will immediately show interest in your words by saying "SURE! HOW CAN I GET SOME OF IT WITHOUT GIVING MUCH IN RETURN?"

One of the very first jobs I ever had was that of handy-boy around a saw-mill, but it gave me a chance to see that a big puffing steam engine turned the machinery; that the steam in the big boiler kept the engine running; that the fireman kept the steam pouring into the engine by

constantly pushing wood into the firebox. I noticed that when the fire began to die down the steam began to die down also; that a hot fire produced plenty of steam. Then and there I got my first lesson, in an elementary sort of way, of the principle of cause and effect. Later in life, long after I had worked myself into a higher place than that of handy-boy around a saw-mill, I saw evidence on every hand that there was a cause for everything; that nothing just happened by mere accident. I saw that achievement in any undertaking depended very largely upon the amount of intelligent effort put into it; that those who achieved most were those who served best.

Source: Napoleon Hill's Magazine, May-June 1923; page 34.

Chapter 6

SEVENTEEN SUCCESS PRINCIPLES

Think and Grow Rich is simply an account of success principles not claimed to be Hill's own, but rather those he compiled from Andrew Carnegie and other successful businessmen of that era. Dr. Hill's teachings have always come from humility, not arrogance. He shares, not lectures.

—RICH WINOGRAD

You do not need a fortune teller, tarot cards, palm reading, or physics to predict your future if you are on Napoleon Hill's road to success. Personal self-analysis can be easily handled by reviewing the Seventeen Success Principles and noting the degree to which you use each one in your daily life. For each of the seventeen principles, you might begin to condition your mind toward consciously using each steppingstone to success by reviewing a principle a day, and when finished with all seventeen begin again.

W. Clement Stone tells us that repetition is the key! Not only does it reinforce what we know, it seeps down into our subconscious minds and programs us for successful habits that are unconscious. The meaning here is that we do not have to consciously think about these habits, because we know them so thoroughly that they are programmed into our brain's hardware and we no longer have to think about engaging them—they just occur. This is powerful programming.

Here are the simple questions in which you will supply the name of the daily principle that you are studying. The Seventeen Success Principles are:

1. Definiteness of Purpose
2. Mastermind Alliance
3. Applied Faith
4. Going the Extra Mile
5. Pleasing Personality
6. Personal Initiative
7. Positive Mental Attitude
8. Enthusiasm
9. Self-Discipline
10. Accurate Thinking
11. Controlled Attention
12. Teamwork
13. Learning from Adversity and Defeat
14. Creative Vision
15. Maintenance of Sound Health
16. Budgeting Time and Money
17. Cosmic Habitforce

You are where you are and what you are because
of your established habits of thought and deed.
—NAPOLEON HILL

Considering each of these principles, take time to answer these questions:

- What does this principle or idea mean to you in your daily life?

- How will you apply this key principle or idea?

- When (note exact time and date) will you start applying this key principle or idea?

- What will you consciously do now that you wouldn't have done had you not studied this principle? Keep a notebook on your written responses to these questions. Note exact actions that you take daily to bring these principles into action in your daily life. The more you DO, the more you will HAVE.

Remember the formula for success: Success = Thought + Emotionalized Action

Your Own Future

Dr. Napoleon Hill

If you are interested in your own future, practically anyone of intelligence can help you read it quite accurately if you will answer these questions:

First: Do you practice the habit of doing more work than you are paid for?

Second: Do you depend upon your own plans and your own efforts for advancement?

Third: Have you trained yourself to do the thing that ought to be done without someone telling you to do it?

Fourth: Do you understand the principle of CAUSE and EFFECT?

Fifth: Do you wait for opportunities to show up, or quietly go about creating them?

Answer these five questions correctly, and even the most elementary thinker can foretell what your finish will be.

You are living in the most advantageous age in the entire history of the world, and regardless of what your present station in life may be or how humble your beginning, the possibilities ahead of you stagger the imagination. You are living in an age that affords every needed stimulant to arouse your imagination and inspire you with ambition.

I am not posing as a competent judge to tell you what you ought to do, but may I suggest that you climb aboard a force that is practically irresistible—a force that will carry you on to the very summit of achievement of the highest order—if you will make it your business and your life work to sow the seeds of friendly cooperation in the hearts of all whom you influence.

Source: Napoleon Hill's Magazine, May-June 1923; page 36.

Chapter 7

THE SUBSTANCE
OF SUCCESS

You have been given a wonderful opportunity. Are you
going to recognize it, seize upon it, and live out your
dreams, or be one of the many poor souls who wonder
what might have been? The choice is yours and yours
alone. I wish each of you nothing but the best.
                                             —DON GREEN

As you study Dr. Hill's teachings, you may be asking
yourself what really is the substance of success. For
each one of us the answer is different. Sometimes it is called
our heart's desire—that internal yearning for something just
beyond our reach, something that is like a dream come true. It
could be the vacation of a lifetime, our children's achievements,
a special relationship, a perfect home that matches our inner
daydreams, recognition of a job well done, and just about
anything that could make our lives complete.

Taking a cue from Napoleon Hill, I would like to suggest that each day you find something in your own life that
parallels Dr. Hill's Twelve Riches of Life. He states, "We can
become masters of ourselves, if we so desire. The main thought

to bear in mind is first to gain the knowledge, and secondly to apply it."

The following are examples as to how to list the riches that Hill discusses and apply them in your own life. Daily, review the twelve points that parallel Dr. Hill's prescription for a healthy, happy, and terrific life! Next, apply them and make them uniquely your own.

Examples: Where can I find this treasure?

1. Positive Mental Attitude: When you awake each morning, recite the affirmation, "I feel healthy, I feel happy, I feel terrific!" Do this several times mentally and even out loud and see how your day goes. Give it time. You might commit to a 30-day trial period.

2. Sound Physical Health: Each day decide to eat healthy choices—at least for the meal you are currently having. No need to plan a month's menu—just remind yourself that you are the custodian of your own health, and that as caregiver you want to always select the best available options each day at every meal.

3. Harmony in Human Relationships: Instead of initiating a disagreement, initiate a solution. Refrain from combative behavior. Work toward collaboration.

4. Freedom from Fear: Little fears can lead to enormous ones. Always remember that faith is the opposite of fear. Act in faith instead of failing to act due to fear.

5. The Hope of Achievement: Inspire yourself by creating a dream of your own to conceive, believe, and achieve.

6. The Capacity for Faith: Stretch your mind to embrace choices made with faith as the backbone to your decision. Soon you could sprout wings!

7. Willingness to Share Your Blessings: Make someone else's day. Focus on being the bearer of goodness instead of the recipient.

8. A Labor of Love: Do something each day that you love to do and would do regardless of the compensation.

9. An Open Mind on All Subjects: Say "yes" to an invitation that you would rather decline because you are not sure you would enjoy it.

10. Self-Discipline: Do a little more, work a little harder, tackle the dreaded task for the sake of showing yourself who is your real boss.

11. The Capacity to Understand People: Learn to enjoy the company of diverse groups of people. Be all-embracing rather than exclusionary.

12. Financial Security: Make setting aside money for a future purpose a game of sorts that represents gratification—but at a later date. Mark savings on a calendar with an ending date and final amount in mind. You are not denying yourself, but rewarding yourself on a designated date.

Remember to look daily for these hidden treasures in your life. Soon it will become second nature, and that is when the true riches will unfold.

Turning Failure into Stepping Stones to Success

Dr. Napoleon Hill

Has it ever occurred to you that every failure and every mistake from which you survive, and every obstacle which you master, develop in you wisdom, strategy, and self-mastery—without which you could accomplish no great undertaking?

No one likes to meet with failure, yet every failure can be turned into a stepping-stone that will carry one to the heights of achievement, if the lessons taught by the failure are organized, classified and used as a guide.

If your failures embitter you toward others and develop cynicism in your heart, they will soon destroy your usefulness; but, if you accept them as necessary teachers and build them into a shield, you can make of them an impenetrable protection.

Vanity prompts us to give more thought to our triumphs than we do to our failures, yet, if we profit by the experience of those who have accomplished most in the world, we will see that a man never needs to watch himself so closely as when he begins to attain success, because success causes a slackening of effort and a letting down of that eternal vigilance which causes a man to throw the power of his combative nature into that which he is doing.

Source: Napoleon Hill's Magazine, February 1922, back cover.

Chapter 8

DEMOLISHING BARRIERS

As this world gets ever smaller, the incidents of shared world experiences are dramatically increasing. This brings us more and more into the awareness that we are not only one nation but one humanity. We are one brotherhood of nations that belong together, not apart.

—URIEL MARTINEZ

The Irish are famous for their beautiful stone walls that grace the Emerald Isle and make the countryside appear like a patchwork quilt when viewed from the air. These stone walls or fences are constructed without any mortar and are so intricately assembled that they endure for decades, some even centuries. When driving in Ireland on the narrow roads, a person can literally reach out and touch these walls. Because they traditionally serve many purposes, they are loved by visitors and citizens alike. These walls separate but do not segregate; they divide but do not alienate neighbors from one another.

Other types of walls do serve as barriers and should be torn down. These can be real or imaginary walls that do exist to divide and conquer. Their purpose is to mark territory and keep people apart. Walls such as these serve no purpose in our global community. Diversity is an asset and should be cultivated as a method for personal growth. When something new is experienced, we broaden our outlook and learn to embrace new ways of being.

Dr. Hill proposes conquering real and imaginary walls through persistence. Work could present a seemingly insurmountable wall for some, housecleaning for another, and even social duties and obligations for yet a third group. Ask yourself what walls you have constructed in your life. Why allow these walls to confine you? Do these walls prevent you from tackling both the big and small jobs that would enable you to grow as a person? Then, why do you maintain them? Be persistent and tear them down! Mentally decide that you will not be restrained by artificial barriers and remove those walls.

Walls that draw you in and embrace you in an aesthetic sense like those in Ireland can enrich our lives. Walls that exclude and separate one from another only strengthen barriers and boundaries. Which ones will you permit to exist in your mental landscape? For those you want to remove, how will you now begin the demolition?

Stone Walls

Dr. Napoleon Hill

You are an unusual person if you never came to what seemed to be a stone wall that stood between you and achievement.

Lately I have been studying the lives of Lincoln, Socrates, Plato, Napoleon and some of the more modern men of achievement, and it encourages me to discover that every one of these men found not one, but many such stone walls between him and his goal.

In my own somewhat commonplace career, I have encountered many of these stone walls. When I see one of them in front of me I walk up to it and test it with a hammer to make sure that it is not made of mere clay. If I find it to be real stone, I then bring up a step-ladder and proceed to climb over it. If I find a spiked fence on top, I climb down again and proceed to the right, believing that the wall cannot possibly extend around the earth. If I find the way blocked, I turn to the left, hoping to find a passage-way in that direction. If I find the road blocked in that direction, I then begin to dig a tunnel under the wall, for it blocks my pathway to achievement and I have to pass!

If I find the wall built on solid rock and no tunnel is possible, I then resort to the last means of disposing of the wall, by applying a strong charge of TNT and blowing the thing out of the way. The TNT is also known under another name—Persistence, the twelfth rung of the Magic Ladder to Success.

Source: Napoleon Hill's Magazine, May-June 1923, page 12.

Chapter 9

THE END OF THE RAINBOW

I was emotionally devastated by events which left me confused, scared and, worst of all, humbled by doubts about my capability to attain success. Yet in hindsight each of these temporary defeats (although at the time they sure seemed permanent) led me to something even better in my life...now I look back and laugh!
— JIM ROHRBACH

The process of learning from our past mistakes is one of life's lessons that can assist us in turning the corner to success. Although the lessons can be the most difficult ones of our lives, these lessons can also be the most enduring. If we condition our minds to look for the seed of an equal or greater benefit when an "adversity" occurs, we begin the process of moving away from the negativity of the situation. This is not easily done, but it is the most beneficial thing that we can do given the circumstances.

As you read the following article by Dr. Hill, you can readily see how he reviews the adversities that occurred in his life and how he repositioned himself on his path to riches. We must do the same thing in our lives if we are going to continue the upward climb rather than the downward spiral. This is a recurring theme in Dr. Hill's philosophy and a very important one, because unless we are willing to capitalize on our mistakes or so-called failures, we will never understand how the Universe is handing us the substance of success within the seed that we are told to locate.

Once this seed is located, the choice then becomes ours. We are given free will by Infinite Intelligence, and if and when we choose to use it, the outcome then ultimately is in our hands. "Thoughts are things." As we think on good thoughts rather than negative happenings, we begin to open up an entire universe that is at our service.

Why not take a moment today and review some of the adversities in your life that held seeds for growth? These could be the very seeds that you need to plant now for your growth and development. At a certain time of year we often hear the phrase, "Think spring!" Well, now I challenge you not only to "Think spring," but "Think harder!" Grow where you are planted.

The End of the Rainbow

Dr. Napoleon Hill

First, and most important of all, in my search for the rainbow's end I found God in a very concrete, unmistakable and satisfying manifestation, which is quite sufficient if I had found nothing more. All my life I had been somewhat unsettled in my own mind as to the exact nature of that Unseen Hand which directs the affairs of the universe, but my seven turning-points on the rainbow trail of life brought me, at last, to a conclusion which satisfied. Whether or not my conclusion is right or wrong is not of much importance; the main thing is that it satisfied me.

The lessons of lesser importance which I learned are these:

I learned that those whom we consider our enemies are, in reality, our friends. In the light of all that has happened I would not begin to go back and undo a single one of those trying experiences with which I met, because each one of them brought me positive evidence of the soundness of the Golden Rule and the existence of the law of compensation through which we claim our rewards for virtue and pay the penalties for our ignorance.

I learned that Time is the friend of all who base their thoughts and actions on Truth and Justice, and, that it is the mortal enemy of all who fail to do so, even though the penalty or the reward is often slow in arriving where it is due.

I learned that the only pot of gold worth striving for is that which comes from the satisfaction of knowing that one's efforts are bringing happiness to others.

One by one I have seen those who were unjust and who tried to destroy me, cut down by failure. I have lived to see every one of them reduced to failure far beyond anything that they planned for me. The banker whom I mentioned was reduced to poverty; the men who stole my interest in the Betsy Ross Candy Company and tried to destroy my reputation have come down to what looks to be permanent failure, one of them being a convict in the federal prison.

The man who defrauded me out of my $100,000 salary, and whom I elevated to wealth and influence, has been reduced to poverty and want. At every turn of the road which led, finally, to my rainbow's end, I saw undisputable evidence to back the Golden Rule philosophy which I am now sending forth, through organized effort, to hundreds of thousands of people.

Lastly, I have learned to listen for the ringing of the bell which guides me when I come to the cross-roads of doubt and hesitancy. I have learned to tap a heretofore unknown source from which I get my promptings when I wish to know which way to turn and what to do, and these promptings have never led me in the wrong direction and I am confident they never will.

As I finish these lines I see, on the walls of my study, the pictures of great men whose characters I have tried to emulate. Among them is that of the immortal Lincoln, from whose rugged, care-worn face I seem to see a smile emerging and from whose lips I can all but hear those magic words, "With charity for all and malice toward none," and deep down in my heart I hear the mysterious bell ringing and following it comes, once more, as I close these lines, the greatest message that ever reached my consciousness: "Standeth God within the shadow of every failure."

Source: *Napoleon Hill's Magazine,* September 1921; pages 38, 48.

Chapter 10

INCH BY INCH
IT'S A CINCH

Many Japanese seem to abide by Applied Faith, although every Japanese has not studied his Seventeen Principles. That is, Applied Faith is a universal principle of achievement beyond national boundaries. In my view, there seems a tacit understanding among the Japanese, in spite of this time of unprecedented crisis, or because of this time of unprecedented crisis, that we must use Applied Faith.

—KIYOTAKA HARAI

Have you ever been at a loss for words? Situations that are overwhelming and nightmarish can padlock our mouths and leave us speechless. As we consider an appropriate response—any response—we discard each one because there is no response that could possibly bandage a wound as gaping as the Grand Canyon. So, that leaves us with few alternatives except putting ourselves in a "do nothing" position. As we cower in the corner of grief, action seems like the last thing that would bring healing. Yet, without action nothing happens.

Faith without works is dead. Hope cannot heal unless it is actualized and brought into the here and now.

Looking at recent global events causes most people to feel depressed and helpless. The enormity of the situations seemingly prevents any single individual from making a profound difference. Yet, if everyone thought this way the outcome could become even more hellish. In my opinion, it is better to light one candle than to curse the darkness. Pick up one piece of litter, rather than fault the government for dirty towns. Donate a reasonable amount to a charity, rather than saying a small donation cannot do any good. Instead of lamenting what can't be done, do something directed toward creating a good outcome, and leave it to the universal law of cause and effect to make a difference. In the meantime, others may begin to model your behavior and create a larger movement that can and will have a greater impact. Inch by inch it's a cinch. Yard by yard it's hard. Take healing actions one step at a time.

Do something today that is positive. Don't just think it—do it. Ask your conscience what immediate small actions you can take right now that will improve your environment. Next, to restate a saying, walk your thoughts. This is a real alternative that can begin the healing process. Won't you take that one small step that can begin the movement toward a brighter future for everyone? Of course you will. Do it now.

November Eleventh!

Dr. Napoleon Hill

There is no death! The stars go down
To rise upon some fairer shore;
And bright in Heaven's jeweled crown
They shine forever more.
There is no death! The leaves may fall,
And flowers may fade and pass away;
They only wait, through wintry hours,
The coming of the May.

If there is a crime in all the world that causes the all-seeing God to tremble with pity and angels to weep with grief and the planets of the universe to go out of their accustomed paths, it is the crime of wholesale murder, called war!

On November the eleventh we are reminded of the most destructive war the world has ever witnessed; a war that sent millions of human souls into eternity. Let us stop, today, and take inventory of civilization's gain from that war.

On the debit side of the ledger let us write the tragic story of pestilence and famine which is sweeping over Russia like a mighty tornado; and the story of intolerance and hate that has been written on the hearts of the people of every nation engaging in that war; and the famine that swept over China like a beast of prey, cutting down millions of innocent human beings; and here in our own beloved America, where the results of the inventory are more impressive because all who will look may see the effects, let us add to the indictment against this monster called war, the story of idle factories and unemployed men and disturbed relationship between employer and employee. And, on the credit side of the inventory—what?

Absolutely nothing—nothing except unimpeachable evidence that war is a game of murder in which the winner is also the loser. Today, as we mourn the loss of those American boys who sleep beneath the sod in Flanders fields, let us petition the Almighty king in one concentrated, unbroken line of prayer, and ask that the emissaries to the disarmament conference soon to be held in Washington may never leave these shores or set foot on their native soil again until they shall have pledged themselves and their peoples to the task of making another world war impossible by destroying the implements of war and by filling the hearts of their peoples with the love of God, through organized education, so they will never again tolerate war. In the name of God, Amen!

> *No North, no South, no East, no West,*
> *But one great nation Heaven blest.*
> *No Jew or Gentile, no race or creed,*
> *Just more love of God is all we poor mortals need.*
> —NAPOLEON HILL

Source: *Napoleon Hill's Magazine,* November 1921; page 6.

Chapter 11

RECOGNIZE THE
VALUE OF OTHERS

We all know we have things to work on that might benefit both ourselves and the people we spend our time with, but it's hard to put the effort into making adjustments. The risk we run with not making the adjustments is that the outcome can be way more labor intensive (and painful) than the alternative.

—ROBIN BYRD POWELL

April 1st, or April Fool's Day, is a good time to reflect on the idea of how a person might make another look or feel foolish rather than in control. It is simply not in good taste to make others the brunt of a joke. If the tables were reversed, you would not enjoy having someone take advantage of you in this manner. Light-heartedness and mean-spiritedness are not the same sides of a coin.

How do you know if you have crossed the line by being disrespectful to another person? The easiest way to determine whether you are being disrespectful is to reverse roles and ask yourself if you would enjoy it as much if you were the recipient of your action. Good, clean fun is one approach to earning a hearty laugh, but vindictive humor is making yourself look good at another's expense. What appears "funny" to one person may appear cruel to another.

Pranks and jokes played on others in grade school to solicit laughter are juvenile and not in good taste. Usually the intention is to harm or embarrass someone. When all is said and done, the after effects of the joke may rebound on the jokester. Mutual laughter is contagious as in the case when someone gets the giggles and is unable to stop laughing. Young girls are prone to this type of laughter especially in church or at a somber event such as a wake or funeral. In reality, this is a way of dispelling the heavy mood which if maintained could lead to depression. Laughter can be a response that brings a person back to a normal range of feeling.

Laughter can tickle the soul or it can escalate feelings of incompetence and low self-esteem. Why not solicit laughter by giving the unexpected compliment that reminds a person of their real worth? Valuing and respecting individuals for their true worth might just rebound on you in a good way. What goes around comes around, right?

So on the next April Fool's Day, why not have the joke be on the fact that you intend to make people blush from praise through recognition of their good points, rather than blush from being made to look foolish? Give it a try. And then engage in some soul-tickling laughter: that is a good way to open the door to lasting friendships.

You Can Move Mountains When You Learn to...Recognize the Value of Others

Dr. Napoleon Hill

The most intense yearning of every normal person is for recognition of his value and worth as an individual human being.

More than money, more than fame, more than any material thing, this is the greatest reward you can give anyone—to let people know that you appreciate them for themselves alone, rather than for what they can do for you.

Humanity's fate in this existence is, in essence, a lonely one. Except for faith in the Creator, each is born alone and dies alone. Although it may be possible to postpone someone's death through our own sacrifice, no one actually can die for another.

Each ultimately faces the end of earthly existence as a matter strictly between the person and God. It is this subconscious realization that causes us our essential loneliness, that causes us to strive so mightily for the appreciation of others.

Psychiatrists and psychologists are coming to realize, as philosophers and priests have realized for centuries, that this is the basic drive of humankind—not sex, or the urge for security, but the demand for simple, egotistical recognition.

None of us has so long to live that we can afford to waste a precious moment in such a negative way as carping criticisms of others. But every moment spent in praise of someone else rebounds to our own credit. For nowhere is it more true that like begets like than in this instance.

That doesn't mean that you must engage in fatuous flattery or apple polishing. Nor does it meant that you must overlook errors and ineptness in subordinates.

But it does mean that every word of criticism you offer should be given in a spirit of helpful instructiveness, with a view to making the subject a better person, a better worker, than he was before. It also means that you are willing to recognize the good points as well as the bad and give them greater weight of appreciation.

It will help you, too, to remember than no man or woman is entirely free of the drive for recognition. That includes your superiors as well as your subordinates. Your boss at this moment is probably more tired, more lonely, and more disheartened than you realize. He would appreciate a word of sincere praise from you every bit as much as the one you hope to receive from him or her.

As a matter of tactfulness, too, beware of the person who invites you to "Go ahead and criticize me. I want your honest opinion." Few of us are so self-disciplined that we actually enjoy criticism. Such an invitation is merely a sign of a person's need for recognition. Humankind's greatest punishment for miscreants lies not in the bars and strict discipline of prison life. It's in the eradication of the prisoner's individuality—the uniforms, the numbers, the deliberate withdrawal of recognition.

The true leader in the military service carefully guards the individual ego of each subordinate. Although realizing the need for discipline and uniformity, a leader also realizes the inherent dangers they hold as killers of personality and spirit. Hence, the true leader makes sure that every person knows they are valued and respected as an individual.

By adopting the same attitude, you will be taking a tremendous step toward becoming a leader yourself.

Source: Adapted from *Success Unlimited,* April 1966; pages 33-34.

Chapter 12

FEAR NOT

Sadly, the self-help doctrine has been hijacked by a movement called the prosperity gospel—i.e., preachers who say that God wants you to be rich. Faith, self-help and prosperity are noble words and should not be conceded to the hucksters. My simple faith is this: If we are created in God's image, then we were born to create, and to create is to prosper.

—RICH KARLGAARD

M any people believe that we are spiritual beings having a human experience. If this is true, and I believe it is, is it any wonder that when we are tapped on the shoulder with a spiritual message that we sit up and take notice? Well, that type of personally delivered message doesn't happen every day, but when it does we can become startled into awareness. Awareness of the life we are given and are put here to live shouldn't come as a shock to any of us, but too often many of us tread the path of least resistance and are satisfied with our little lot in life.

Napoleon Hill was spiritual in his approach, but intentionally non-denominational when it came to declaring his espoused system of personalized religious beliefs. I believe that he did this for a purpose. And that purpose would be to create an all-embracing philosophy of success that didn't exclude people because of their spiritual inclinations. Hill was spiritual in insight demonstrated by the values and beliefs that permeate his Seventeen Success Principles, but not small-minded in his approach to advancing his philosophy. Instead of alienating people, Dr. Hill wanted to create a global community operating under the same unifying principles of success.

So, by not openly declaring his specific religious affiliation, he left the door open for others to enter. His "Infinite Intelligence" and "Cosmic Habitforce" explanations of universal laws of cause and effect allow for various systems of belief to fall under one big canopy of thought. After all, humankind is not separated into various subspecies or lesser categories. We are all one and the same. We are born, mature, grow old, and die. This is everyone's lot in life. However, what we make of the experience determines our personalized outcome for good or ill.

Dr. Hill always strove to go above and beyond the norm. Whether he was debating Hitler or the devil himself, no opponent was too outrageous to be engaged. During these "conversations," Dr. Hill considers the evils that can be pervasive in society if the causes of failure run rampant. Then, as a counterpoint, Dr. Hill offers the only known solution to societal ills—the Science of Success. And it works every single time that you work it.

Fear

Dr. Napoleon Hill

Fear is the greatest single obstacle to success.

Too often, people let fear rule all their decisions and actions.

Their every yearning is for a sort of overall protection summed up in the catch-all cliché of "security."

The truly successful person doesn't think in these terms. The successful person's reasoning is based on creativeness and productivity. As former President Eisenhower said, "One can attain a high degree of security in a prison cell if that's all he wants out of life."

The successful person is one who is willing to take risks when sound logic shows they are necessary to reach the desired goal.

All of us suffer from fear. What is it? Fear is an emotion intended to help preserve our lives by warning us of danger. Hence, fear can be a blessing when it raises its flag of caution so we pause and study a situation before making a decision or taking action.

We must control fear rather than permit it to control us. Once it has served its emotional purpose as a warning signal, we must not permit it to enter into the logical reasoning by which we decide upon a course of action.

FDR's [U.S. President Franklin D. Roosevelt's] famous words—"We have nothing to fear but fear itself "—are as applicable now, and at any time, as when he uttered them during the Depression.

How can you overcome your fears? First of all, by looking them full in the face—by consciously saying: "I am afraid." And then asking yourself: "Of what?"

With that one question you have begun analyzing the situation facing you. You are on the road of reason that will carry you around the emotional obstacle of fear.

The next step is to consider the problem from every facet. What are the risks? Is the expected reward worth taking them? What are the other possible courses of action? What unexpected problems are likely to be encountered? Do you have all the necessary data, statistics and facts at hand? What have others done in similar situations, and what were the results?

Once you have completed your study, take action—immediately!

Procrastination leads only to more doubt and fear.

A noted psychologist once said that a woman, alone at night and imagining she hears noises, can settle her fears quickly. All she has to do is put one foot on the floor. In doing so, she has taken the first step on a positive course of action toward overcoming her fear.

People seeking success must force themselves in the same way to control their fear by taking the first step toward their goal.

And remember that no one walks the road of life alone.

One of the most consoling—and truest—assurances given us is found in the Bible: "Fear not, I am with you always."

Faith in those words will give you spiritual strength to meet any situation.

Source: Adapted from *Success Unlimited,* October 1966, pages 33-34.

Chapter 13

CULTIVATE CREATIVE VISION

There exist many excellent definitions of creativity, but what defines a creative individual? This person... is flexible when thinking—able to go here, there, everywhere...is enthusiastic about life...frolics in the playground of the imagination...and above all, gardens a positive mental attitude!

—Daniel Yovich

One way that a person can use creative imagination is in the purposeful planning for peace. Everywhere we are bombarded with signs and symbols of aggravation, dissension, and indicators of aggression that ultimately lead to war. What makes it so, and how can one person ultimately make a difference?

Driving to work yesterday, I actively looked for the usual signs of spring that herald the season of renewal in northwest Indiana. Returning robins, budding pussywillows, longer days, and greening grass are all present for the viewing. These harbingers come naturally and when they return, almost an audible sigh of relief is heard indicating that spring is once again in the works.

But, yesterday I noticed man-made beauty too. Some yards have flower beds that display yellow daffodils that add beauty to residences. Some neighbors are collecting litter that has accumulated over the winter and are tidying up their spots on the planet. Dead leaves are being raked up and bagged for disposal. As the outdoors is spruced up, evidence of interior cleaning is occurring too. This caused me to wonder what would happen if everyone did the following:

1. Construct and maintain a flower bed with seasonal blooms that passersby could enjoy—sort of like eye candy for the soul. Wouldn't some people slow down and admire the festival of colors? Friendly competition could occur as one neighbor learns from and imitates another. Growing the best morning glories, marigolds, zinnias, four-o'clocks, roses, hollyhocks, petunias, pansies, moonflowers, etc., could replace our attraction to the gore of the daily news. Seeds can be cultivated and shared over a cup of coffee or tea. Just think of the beauty and the small cost of creating such wonder! What can you construct with a shovel, soil, seeds, and self? Go for it. Make someone's day this way!

2. In Ireland, communities are recognized for being "Tidy Towns." As you enter a town, a large congratulatory sign is displayed indicating the award and the year it was received. When seen, this sends a message that the town respects the environment, and people tend not to litter because the town openly displays the value of being clean.

Driving to work I can count by blocks the road kill that litters the streets in various forms of decomposition along the highways I travel. Cats, dogs, deer, raccoons, possums, skunks, fowl, rats, and even turtles are daily reminders of life's untidy consequences. Probably on my daily 30-mile, one-way commute, I can count without trying 30-40 carcasses along my path. Not too pleasant of a sight. Why not tidy up, or have town management offer this service for a fee? Does not this view of our environment negatively color our perception of the world?

3. If each of us took care of our allotted space on this planet by making an attempt to beautify it, wouldn't the world take on a better appearance little by little? Ralph Waldo Emerson states that the "Earth laughs in flowers." Gandhi says, "Be the change that you want to see in the world." "Each one teach one" is a good way to begin. It doesn't take much creative imagination to shove a spade into the earth and plant some seeds. But it does take the Creator to manifest the outpouring of new life. Are you ready to be a harbinger of spring and beauty? Plant for today, bloom for tomorrow, and decide right now to make a positive statement for improvement, not perfection, in the here and now.

The Ladder of Success Is Never Crowded at the Top

Dr. Napoleon Hill

People with creative vision know that they can succeed only by helping others succeed, and they know also that it is not necessary for another to fail in order that they may succeed.

The person with creative vision produces results instead of alibis. If they make mistakes, as all do, they are not afraid to accept the responsibility for them, and never try to shift that responsibility to another.

These creative people make decisions quickly, but changes them just as readily when they discover that they have made the wrong decision. They have no fear of others, either of higher or lower rank than themselves, for they are at peace with their own conscience, is fair with others, and honest.

These are some of the traits of character of which creative vision is born.

These are plain words, but people of sound character and creative vision relish plain speaking.

One of the common weaknesses of most of us is that we look with envy at people who have attained noteworthy success, taking stock of them during the hour of their triumph without taking note of the price each had to pay for success. And we erroneously believe that they owe their success to some sort of pull, luck, or dishonesty. Personal achievement, power, fame, and riches: each has a definite price, and the person with creative vision not only knows the price but is willing to pay it.

The person with creative vision understands the benefits of sharing blessings, experiences, and opportunities with others, recognizing that only by this method can he or she attain and enjoy enduring prosperity, happiness and the respect of others.

The person with creative vision also understands that combined creative vision of several minds, directed toward a definite end in a spirit of harmony, is the very heart of the master mind principle and that this type of creative vision is a tremendous source of power.

Source: Adapted from *PMA: Science of Success,* Educational Edition, Napoleon Hill Foundation, 1983; pages 419-420.

Chapter 14

POSITIVE ATTITUDE ATTRIBUTES

As I exited the plane I gave my flight attendant, Marie, a note. It said, "Excellent customer service, with a sincere smile, is a talent and a special gift. Thanks for what you do." Thanks to Napoleon Hill and Judy Williamson for their teachings. Without it I probably would have exited that plane complaining about something insignificant like the small bag of peanuts I had for lunch.

—RICH WINOGRAD

Cultivating a positive mental attitude is like acquiring a taste for a new food. At first, whatever is introduced to you may seem too outrageous, too unusual for your normal preferences. But over time, as you are introduced to a new item you may find that what you used to avoid you now seek out. Like a baby being introduced to soft foods for the first time, initial rejection probably occurs. Later, however, the applesauce, peas, and peaches taste pretty good.

In all forms of learning we are like babies being exposed to new ideas and choices. Sometimes rejection occurs even before the trial period begins. People state, "I know I won't like it, so why bother?" But how do you really know if you won't try it?

As we mature, our tastes change. Once I listened as a friend related the contents of a sandwich that she loved as a child. I had the ingredients, so I offered to make her one for lunch, but she said, "No, thank you. I would rather live with the memory than be disappointed." Memories can inspire us to action but they can also hold us back. If we decide that nothing will ever match up with something from our past, then we have already closed our minds. But, on the other hand, if we cherish our early memories but move forward toward new experiences, we have the best of both worlds.

What inspires you to action? What motivates you to try new things? What brings fullness and satisfaction into your daily routine? These are the things to be coaxed forward for a rich life. Try something new. Like a good cup of coffee, life should be full-brewed and aromatic. A daily diet of leftovers would be stale and boring, and so is a person who cultivates no new experiences.

Decide to experience one new thing each day. This could be a new food, friendship, or foreign phrase. After all, isn't that the purpose of life? Be green and supple, rather than discolored and decayed.

Positive Mental Attitude Attributes

Dr. Napoleon Hill

Form the habit of tolerance and keep an open mind on all subjects, toward people of all races and creeds. Learn to like people just as they are, instead of demanding of them that they be as you wish them to be.

Avoid the fear of old age by remembering that the Creator so blessed humankind that nothing is ever taken from us without something of equal or greater value given in return. Through the operation of this profound plan, youth is replaced by wisdom. It may help you to accept and appreciate this truth if you are reminded that the greatest achievements usually take place after we are well beyond the age of fifty.

Let your motto be: Deeds, not mere words.

Source: *PMA: Science of Success,* Educational Edition, Napoleon Hill Foundation, 1983.

Chapter 15

ACCURATE THINKERS

What you can't fall victim to is negative thinking. That only leads to deflated attitudes, less activity, and poor sales skills. It tends to feed itself and you start looking for reasons to fail, and you often find them!

—MIKE BROOKS

For some, the word "custodian" can take on a meaning of an employee who works at a menial job for the standard hourly rate.

In one sense of the word, this can be accurate. Still, if we look deeper, the meaning of custodian has greater relevancy. Someone who is a custodian is guarding or overseeing something that is precious. Unless what is to be guarded is of value, no one would concern themselves with putting someone in charge of looking after it. Whether you are the custodian of a child, a custodian of the faith, or the custodian of a building, you are the keeper of a precious commodity that should not be abused. To be a custodian is to be in the position of great trust. The job description requires that you care for whatever you are in charge of as if it were your own.

Potential problems can occur when custodians assume that what they have been charged to care for is their personal property. For example, someone who reads and internalizes Dr. Hill's philosophy might assume that the ideas expressed in his works are theirs because the ideas so resonate with them. Next thing you know, they become self-appointed disciples of the system and pronounce themselves trainers, teachers, instructors, seers, or whatever and put themselves in a position of self-appointed authority. Again, there is nothing wrong with aspiring to greatness, but a true leader needs to have the earned credentials behind his or her name. Many people again misunderstand the word "custodian" and soon this designation can morph into the word "charlatan."

Napoleon Hill reminds us that in order to verify someone's claims, the simple question, "How do you know?" can be asked until you get to the bottom of your search. By asking someone this simple question, you retrace the steps leading to their current claim to fame. Next, you as "researcher" need to do your homework too. Verify the answers given by the person in question. Determine if the person has the credentials, training, and education that you aspire to have yourself by doing a background check. You wouldn't go to a "doctor" for an ailment if they were self-appointed rather than AMA-certified, and you should not seek advice from someone other than a person who has been educated in the path that you desire to tread.

So, first put yourself in the position of custodian and learn all you can in order to become what you aspire to be. Your higher self is waiting for you by positioning you in the direction of good choices. This is a path that you must walk alone. No one can do it for you. There are guides, but if you view these guides as billboards offering their wares for a price, you will make better choices. Know that it is your own choice and action that leads you to your destination. As custodian of your talents, your gifts, and the very precious commodity of *you,* let no one assume to tell you the best route for you to take. Only by trekking yourself can you reach your ultimate destination free of any strings attached. To paraphrase Dr. Hill, put yourself in the position of power and only accept someone's opinion and guidance when you can verify their personal credibility. Life is a series of choices. Be guided to make good ones.

Opinions

Dr. Napoleon Hill

Opinions: Everyone except the accurate thinker has an overabundance of opinions, and usually these are without great value. Many of them can also be dangerous and destructive when used in conjunction with personal initiative because if they are based upon bias, prejudice, intolerance, ignorance, guesswork, or hearsay evidence, they may do a great deal of harm.

No opinion can be considered safe unless it is based upon known facts, and no one should express an opinion on any subject without assurance that it is founded on facts, or sound hypotheses of facts. Free advice volunteered by friends and acquaintances usually is not worthy of consideration. The accurate thinker, therefore, never acts upon such advice without giving it the closest scrutiny. Accurate thinkers permit no one to do their thinking for them. They obtain facts, information, and counsel from others, but they retain the privilege of accepting or rejecting such advice in whole, or in part.

Accurate thinkers do not form opinions based upon newspaper reports, for they cannot be sure that such information is always the result of accurate thinking. When someone says to them, "I see by the papers..." they immediately understand that the speaker has an opinion which may or may not be based upon fact, and they do not allow themselves to be influenced solely by what such a person says.

Source: *PMA: Science of Success,* Educational Edition, Napoleon Hill Foundation, 1983; pages 299-300.

Chapter 16

LAUNCHING DREAMS

In 2008 I decided to invest in the Napoleon Hill Foundation self-study program, with the hope that I would learn even more than I had on my own. I was also hoping to gain different perspectives on the materials and to meet some new people who understood the Science of Success even better than I did. Boy did my investment pay off!

—SCOTT SPANBAUER

Action is the one key ingredient that is lacking in many "magical" success formulas. "Wishing, hoping, thinking, praying" is a partial line from a song you may remember. Both in the song's lyrics and in reality this lukewarm approach brings no immediate results. Not until you intensify the action and blend it with a high degree of emotion do you ignite the spark of desire that in turn produces action. From a spark to a flame to a bonfire is not a single step, but the progression is a given if the desire and fuel are present.

In order to bring about a positive result, you must first hold your intention mentally as a thought form, and next, utilizing your physical nature, bring your thought into reality through overt action. Daydreaming, or thinking endlessly about the good life, only produces procrastination and eventually stillborn ideas. But if you bring your ideas to fruition, you can "birth" those ideas into your physical reality by acting on your heart's desire.

Think back to a time when you wanted something in your life that may have been impractical, costly, or beyond your current ability to acquire. Even though you knew that you had roadblocks, the desire wouldn't leave you. Instead of giving up, you revved up your emotional engine and set your course on what it was that you desired with all your heart and soul. As your emotions intensified regarding your desire, so too did your physical self contribute to defining and walking the steps toward reaching your goal.

Dreams are impractical only when we fail to grasp their application in the here and now. Both our waking dreams and our sleeping dreams can forecast our future. The test is not if we fully understand their meanings, but if we understand how to use the received messages for advancement to our higher selves.

How to Get Dreams Off the Launching Pad

Dr. Napoleon Hill

A burning desire to be and to do is the starting point from which the dreamer must take off. Dreams are not born of indifference, laziness, or lack of ambition.

Remember that all who succeed in life get off to a bad start, and pass through many heartbreaking struggles before they "arrive." The turning point in the lives of those who succeed usually comes at the moment of some crisis, through which they are introduced to their "other selves." John Bunyan wrote *The Pilgrim's Progress,* which is among the finest of all English literature, after he had been confined in prison and sorely punished because of his views

on the subject of religion.

O. Henry discovered the genius which slept within his brain after he had met with great misfortune, and was confined in a prison cell, in Columbus, Ohio. Being forced, through misfortune, to become acquainted with his "other self," and to use his imagination, he discovered himself to be a great author instead of a miserable criminal and outcast. Charles Dickens began by pasting labels on blacking pots. The tragedy of his first love penetrated the depths of his soul and converted him into one of the world's truly great authors. That tragedy produced, first, *David Copperfield,* then a succession of other works that made this a richer and a better world for all who read his books.

Helen Keller became deaf, dumb, and blind shortly after birth. Despite her greatest misfortune, she has written her name indelibly in the pages of the history of the great. Her entire life has served as evidence that no one ever is defeated until defeat has been accepted as a reality.

Robert Burns was an illiterate country lad. He was cursed by poverty, and grew up to be a drunkard in the bargain. The world was made better for his having lived, because he clothed beautiful thoughts in poetry, and thereby plucked a thorn and planted a rose in its place.

Beethoven was deaf, Milton was blind, but their names will last as long as time endures, because they dreamed and translated their dreams into organized thought.

There is a difference between wishing for a thing and being ready to receive it. No one is ready for a thing until the person believes it can be acquired. The state of mind must be belief, not mere hope or wish. Open-mindedness is essential for belief. Closed minds do not inspire faith, courage, and belief.

Remember, no more effort is required to aim high in life, to demand abundance and prosperity, than is required to accept misery and poverty.

Source: Adapted from *Think and Grow Rich* by Napoleon Hill, Ballantine Books, NY, August 1966; pages 39-40.

Chapter 17

VALUES DETERMINE ACTIONS

*If you focus on being the person who will do the right
things, you can have anything you want. If you focus
on having things, you are setting yourself up for a life
of frustration.*

—JIM STOVALL

The process of having can either be simple or complex.
Things may come to us out of the thin air as if they were
gifted from the Universe and other things make take a lifetime
to appear.

Whether it is a home, a car, a swimming pool, or a
high-speed boat, these things usually do not show up on our
doorstep overnight and prepaid. Other gifts, however, are as
valuable and free. The fresh scent of lilacs, the greenness of
the grass, air cleansed by rain, the purr of a kitten, the loy-
alty of a dog, the comfortable feel of a feather pillow, and the
warmth of a room after the outside chill. All these things are
available to everyone and do not have a huge price tag with
accompanying maintenance.

How does a person know which gifts of life to pursue? It is truly a difficult task at first because things seem so necessary for achievement. But achievement shown on the outside doesn't mean that there is spiritual satisfaction on the inside. That's the rub. Balance is needed in order to appreciate all the riches of life and usually the ones that demand the most from us are worth the least when then final accounting comes.

What do you value most? Your new car or your new grandchild? Your new suit or the suit you wore well and then gave to Goodwill? Food hoarded or food shared? Lessons learned or lessons taught—or both? Values determine our actions. Before we act, we need to understand what propels us to act. Good values up front often produce good outcomes in the end. Values direct your highest motives, and motives move you to act. Actions create habits. Why not start at the top and ensure that you have hitched your wagon to the highest star of achievement—both of a personal nature and also that of a steward. Stewardship guarantees that you are looking out equally for yourself and others. The service you render will come back multiplied and you will understand why Napoleon Hill said that you must give before you can get—not from any surplus you may possess, but from what you have right now! That is the real secret of stewardship. Give from your current holdings and you will be guided to future holdings right on schedule.

Oriental Proverb

Dr. Napoleon Hill

Here is an old Oriental proverb: *A journey of a thousand miles begins with one step.* It is difficult to anticipate just how a situation will develop in every detail until you take a step forward and try out your present equipment. Then, if weaknesses appear, you will have clues as to how to strengthen your resources. No scheme or plan is perfect. Perfection is a process, not an end.

A little job well done is the first step towards a bigger one.

If the engineer in a train waited to see the block signals show green all the way to his destination, you may be sure no trains would run. But he doesn't do that; he opens the throttle as soon as he sees one or two green lights lining up and is confident that as the train gains speed and momentum, other lights ahead will flash the GO signal.

And here is a final word about the selection of your aim and objective before we give you the mechanics of how to proceed. You know that you will probably never feel that you are completely ready to start any project. There will always be something else you could do in preparation for your take-off. But if you start where you stand and work with whatever tools you have at hand, other and better goals will reveal themselves as you move forward.

Source: *PMA: Science of Success,* Educational Edition, Napoleon Hill Foundation, 1983; page 41.

Chapter 18

A WEALTHY MINDSET

*One of the biggest myths of success is the one in
which we tell ourselves, "It is possible for others to
create wealth, but not me." And then we recite our
homemade excuses. Excuses such as, "I'm too old."
"It's too late for me to start." "I'm uneducated." "I
don't have the proper background or job training."
And on and on....*

—Vic Conant

The creation of wealth begins with a wealthy mindset. By
using the tools of the Seventeen Success Principles that
Dr. Napoleon Hill wrote about in his extended teachings, each
student is handed the toolkit for success. Each time a desire
turns into a definite major purpose, the success toolkit must
be taken off the shelf, dusted off, and utilized tool by tool.
Imaginary goals and dreams do not count in the manifestation
of wealth until and unless strong foundations are built
underneath them. Building a structure takes time, and so does
the creation of a wealthy mindset.

I consider Vic Conant to be a good friend of mine and
the Napoleon Hill Foundation. We have traveled together to
Japan and to Malaysia as business associates, and I have never

witnessed him without a ready smile or lacking in a kind word or helping hand for those who need his guidance. This is remarkable in an age where social media has overtaken the extended hand and the comforting touch or pleasant words of sincere advice that can only be extended by an individual who lives and breathes his definite major purpose. Vic is one of those truly great people who listens to you and offers helpful advice as a person travels his or her chosen path.

Last week, Christina Chia, founder of Napoleon Hill Associates of Malaysia, and I had lunch with Vic Conant in Chicago. We reminisced about his presentation at the 2007 International Convention in Kuala Lumpur, where Vic shared his story of success with other presenters such as Charlie Tremendous Jones and Bob Proctor. These gentlemen each gave the gift of giving back or service in honor of recognizing the influence that Dr. Napoleon Hill had on their outcomes in life. At lunch we discussed the idea of giving to receive, and how many people are reluctant to "give back" when they have arrived at their personal success.

As I listened to Vic, I felt a warm regard for him because he so freely shared his wisdom and time with us. I felt that we met on common ground, as friends, who had the shared interest of making this world a better place. Although the gift of wisdom and friendship can't be seen, it can surely be felt—a hug or a handshake indicates personal alliances far beyond words.

So as you pursue your wealth mindset, be certain that the people you look up to and want to emulate are people with values you admire. Wealth by itself is a worthless asset unless it is shared and disseminated among people it can benefit. Look to a happy person first before you examine their net worth; in the scheme of things, personal happiness and the ability to extend human kindness toward others are two of the most important riches of life.

Education Is Not a Substitute for Work

Dr. Napoleon Hill

No one can get something for nothing. Everything worth having has a definite price, and that price must be paid. The rules of personal achievement are as definite as the rules of mathematics. If ever there was a true science, it is the science of personal achievement described in the seventeen principles of this philosophy.

You are a student of this philosophy. Therefore you are deprived of alibis for failure, including the grandfather of them all, "I never had an opportunity." You have an opportunity, and it lies in the privilege of availing yourself of the combined knowledge of more than five hundred men of great achievement who have made this philosophy available to you.

What are you going to do with your opportunity?

Success does not require a great amount of knowledge about anything, but it does call for the persistent use of whatever knowledge you may have.

How are you using your time?

How much of it are you wasting, and how are you wasting it?

What are you going to do to stop this waste?

These are the questions which should claim your earnest attention throughout this lesson.

Successful people must know themselves, not as they think they are, but as their habits have made them. Therefore you are requested to take inventory of yourself so that you may discover where and how you are using your time.

Source: *PMA: Science of Success,* Educational Edition, Napoleon Hill Foundation, 1983; pages 460-461.

Chapter 19

"WHAT DO I DO NEXT?" (FEAR OF POVERTY)

One young man was successful in everything that he did; nevertheless, he never made any money. People could not understand why. He was ambitious. He was likable. He had a pleasing personality, but financially, he struggled year after year. Finally this young man had it pointed out to him just what his trouble was. He constantly made the statement, "I can do everything well but make money."

—J. MARTIN KOHE

Thoughts of lack can bring us more of the same. Thoughts of abundance work in the opposite manner. Neither work, however, unless we believe in the reality of these thoughts. In order for something to negatively or positively impact us, we must believe in the outcome. Good or bad, we control the presence of thoughts in our mind. To me, it is amazing that conflicting thoughts cannot be present simultaneously in our consciousness. Once we understand this, then it becomes a process for negating the thought that we do not want present in our awareness. Next, this thought eviction leads to a habit.

Evicting the undesirable thought becomes as mundane as sweeping the floor or dusting the end tables. Focusing on the outcomes that we desire causes us to create our future in advance. Truth in advance is like rocket fuel. It propels us with amazing speed toward our end result.

What do you really desire in life? It has been said that in answering this question a person needs to ponder what makes him or her happy. If you love the outdoors but accept a windowless office for your eight-hours-a-day job because it pays so well, are you advancing or retreating when it comes to your very personal desires? Think about it. Does each and every choice position you closer to or away from your goals? Goals either construct or deconstruct your definite major purpose in life. Are you in the construction business or demolition business? It's for you to decide.

Time is of the essence. We never know when the sands in our hourglass will run out. Why risk taking detours and blind alleys? If our purpose in life is clear, then the road to our destination is revealed. Asking the Universe the simple yet profound question, "What do I do next?" usually keeps us on track. Guidance is there for the asking. The only expectation from the Universe is that you follow the advice by walking your customized itinerary. Not everyone wants to be a butcher, a baker, or a candlestick maker, but for those who do, it would be wise to journey down the road that led others to these professions. Success is not a single day-trip, but the entire tour. Know where you are going before you embark and generally you will arrive right on schedule.

First Basic Fear—Fear of Poverty

Dr. Napoleon Hill

One of the most virulent symptoms developed by a fear of poverty is a lack of ambition. Do you accept whatever life hands out without challenging it? Are you generally lazy—mentally and physically? If so, adopt a positive, driving ambition to vanquish this symptom of the fear of poverty.

Do you fail to make your own decisions, but permit someone else to make them for you? This is a second symptom of the fear of poverty. Do not surrender the most precious gift your Creator has bestowed upon you. Make your own decisions! Take advantage of the blessings of American liberty and become self-determining!

A third subtle symptom of the fear of poverty is the habit of making excuses for your failures. Do you offer alibis as to why others have passed you in the economic race? Do you envy and criticize the success of others?

Often the person who suffers from the fear of poverty lives beyond his or her means, is intemperate in personal habits, lacks poise and self-control, wears a frown or scowl, and continually finds fault with everything and everyone.

Fear of poverty breeds within a person the habit of expecting failure instead of success: a general negative mental attitude. Instead of concentrating on ways to succeed, this person discovers all the reasons why a given plan or program will not work. This person's heroes are "sad sacks" rather than successful men and women. These people are generally pessimistic.

And finally, those suffering from the fear of poverty tend to put things off. They are afraid to assume their responsibilities and to institute the proper action to fulfill their duties in life. Thus they never do today what they feel can just as well be put off until tomorrow. They expect and accept poverty, instead of demanding and receiving riches.

Source: Adapted from *PMA: Science of Success,* Educational Edition, Napoleon Hill Foundation, 1983; page 94.

Chapter 20

CREATE A BETTER YOU
(FEAR OF CRITICISM)

Experience will soon teach you that once a decision is made, the problems and troubles begin to disappear. Even though the decision you make may not be the best one, the mere deciding gives you strength and raises your morale. It's the fear of doing the wrong thing that attracts the wrong thing.

—CLAUDE BRISTOL

Consider the words "constructive criticism." Upon hearing them you may be subjected to a little squirming. Although many people delight in unloading criticism on others, the opinions involved often reflect more on the observer than the person under evaluation. If you listen to criticism that is supposed to help you grow, develop, and improve, oftentimes the path under construction is one laid out by the evaluator, and not defined by yourself. It is a given that if the recommended path is trod, your superior will be happy because his or her plan is now in place.

Napoleon Hill asks us to consider whose life we are living anyway. If it is yours, then you should determine your path's destination. If you have abdicated the role of master of your life, then anyone's plan will do. Think about it. Are you required to justify your existence by marching to another's tune? Or, if your marching orders are still in your head and not in synchronization with your life's plan, do you really have anyone to blame but yourself? Being a good soldier is not the same as being a good leader. Leaders lead and soldiers obey. If it is your decision to be a soldier, then orders from your superiors cannot be overanalyzed or subjected to daily constructive criticism. But if you want to be the captain of *your* life, then you must ask and answer the questions that position you best on your success path.

Deciding to take command of your life is not easy because you must then make decisions for yourself and inherit the consequences of your choices. To do any less is to abandon your leadership position. If your fear of criticism stops you in your success tracks, recognize this and get over it. Second by second, minute by minute, and hour by hour, you determine your future via the choices you make.

Ever think about giving yourself constructive criticism? This up-front and personal approach allows you to get to the very heart of the matter where critical change can occur. Only you can do it and only you can process it. Hire yourself as the devil's advocate and through an intense evaluation, uncover what you already know is holding you back. Next, accept the self-evaluation, and go immediately to work in creating a better you for the sole purpose of self-enhancement. Riches begin within. Within you is a better plan for your ultimate good just waiting to be uncovered.

Second Basic Fear—The Fear of Criticism

Dr. Napoleon Hill

This basic fear of what people will say or think keeps many from developing and presenting ideas which would give them independence if acted upon. Thus fear of criticism robs people of their individuality. It undermines their self-reliance and develops an inferiority complex within.

Often the cruelest critics of everything we do, or plan to do, are our relatives. Therefore, it is necessary to caution you again: Keep your definite major purpose to yourself. Do not express it before those who may seize upon it with criticism and attempt to thwart your ambition to excel your previous efforts.

Parents with good intentions but a limited understanding of human relations often do their children irreparable injury by criticizing them, shaming them, or making fun of them and their childhood dreams of achievement. Teasing an adolescent boy about his girl friends, and vice versa, is very definitely a dangerous practice which may lead to permanent social maladjustment in the case of a sensitive personality.

Strangely enough, criticism is one form of service which nearly everyone renders willingly, and usually without charge or invitation. It is the one type of service with which nearly everyone is very generous.

There is, however, a very significant difference between criticism and constructive suggestions. Often an employee, an associate, or a child needs correction. Some of his or her habits may be unproductive, wasteful, or in bad taste. A well-balanced person will learn to accept constructive suggestion in the spirit in which it is given, and will not brood over mistakes of the past.

The three most obvious symptoms of the fear of criticism are:

1. A desire to keep up with the Joneses. This will prompt you to try to maintain a front in competition with your neighbors, even if it causes you to spend beyond your income.

2. The habit of bragging about your achievements, either real or imaginary. It often happens that a person will cover up feelings of inferiority by boasting, emulating others who are successful, and generally trying to give an impression of superiority.

3. An easy embarrassment. This is occasioned by an inability to express definite decisions, a fear of meeting people, reticence, and lack of self-confidence. It often results in fear of those in higher authority, avoidance of responsibility, and lack of personal initiative.

Fear of criticism is almost as general as fear of poverty. Similarly, it saps initiative and prevents the full play of the imagination, thus undermining two essential ingredients for personal achievement and success.

Source: *PMA: Science of Success,* Educational Edition, Napoleon Hill Foundation, 1983; pages 460-461.

Chapter 21

CHOOSE A HEALTHY LIFESTYLE (FEAR OF ILL HEALTH)

No medicine in my doctor's bag can cure people who have lost their will to live. But getting them interested in life again, making them want to live—that's a powerful medicine, one I love to administer.

—ARNOLD FOX, MD

Ask anyone and they will tell you that they want to be healthy. Conduct an on-the-spot, person-on-the-street interview, and regardless who you ask, nearly 100 percent of the people surveyed will tell you that it is their desire to be healthy, to be happy, and to be terrific! Probe a little further and either ask or observe how most people approach working toward the healthy lifestyle that they claim to want. Examine some of the findings below as you observe and "measure" the results.

1. What time do they rise in the morning? What time do they go to bed at night?

2. What do they consume for their daily diet?

3. What type of exercise do they practice? Does any of it extend beyond normal movement? Do they push themselves to do a little more than they feel capable of doing at the time?

4. What do they claim to have as a passion in life? In other words, what is their definite major purpose? Can you see any passion in their lives?

5. What manner do they have for expressing daily gratitude? Do they have a positive mental attitude, do they pray, do they extend acts of kindness toward others and themselves? Do they give without the expectation of return?

6. Do they consider themselves part of the solution or just part of the problem? In other words, do they attempt to correct wrongs they encounter, or do they just accept what is and move on?

Now, reverse your role, and ask yourself the above questions, noticing yourself "from a distance." If you are healthy, happy, and terrific, you will find that these questions and your responses contribute to your overall well-being. Why? Because you choose to be involved in the life you live. Your purpose is not to be a space holder on the sidelines sitting on the bench.

The reality is each one of us is the MVP in our game of life. Recognize this and treat your health and well-being as the most valuable asset that you possess. Because it is!

Third Basic Fear—Fear of Ill Health

Dr. Napoleon Hill

The third basic fear, the fear of ill health, is related to another fear which comes later in the series: the fear of death. Ill health brings one near death sometimes, so the social and physical heredities of a person tend to develop this fear.

The habits of acting and thinking in accordance with the custom or social patterns of behavior to which a person falls heir, by reason of membership in a particular culture, are the person's social heredity.

The actual physical body one receives at birth, with whatever inherent weaknesses and tendencies toward disease it may have, comprise physical heredity.

There is overwhelming evidence that a disease can originate from a negative thought which the person continues to sell internally through auto-suggestion, until the physical symptoms of that disease actually occur within the person. Many medical doctors agree that there is a definite relationship between the patient's mental attitude and his or her physical condition. If this be so, then it follows that you can guarantee yourself sound physical health consciousness whereby you expect, demand, and receive health-sustaining elements from your food, the fresh air, and sunshine!

Source: Adapted from *PMA: Science of Success,* Educational Edition, Napoleon Hill Foundation, 1983; pages 97-98.

Chapter 22

HOPE REPLACES EMPTINESS (FEAR OF LOSS OF LOVE)

Hope replaces the emptiness that adversity leaves behind. Hope can expand to equal and then exceed the adversity that it replaces—if only we believe.
—JUDY WILLIAMSON

Whenever you focus on lack, lack is what you create. Thinking about the loss of love can cause a serious depression to occur in your life. Why not, instead, focus on creating new and rewarding relationships? When latent friendships are cultivated, these newcomers in our lives may not replace old friendships, but they do begin to fill the void that is left.

Napoleon Hill reminds us that the Universe discounts two things: inactivity and a vacuum. If you fail to use it you lose it, and an empty space doesn't stay empty for long before it is filled up with something. These are two natural laws of the Universe that Dr. Hill relates as examples to encourage you to take personal initiative in your own life before someone decides to move in and do it for you.

If you are a mover and a shaker, then you need to act on your definite major purpose in life. There are no sideline routes to success. You must travel the main road, or get run over. Likewise, when a space exists in your life, you need to determine how you are going to fill it. At graduation, commencement speakers many times challenge graduates to become lifelong learners, because these speakers know that a void has been created when a person graduates. Some graduates vow never to crack open another book while others decide to continue to grow through formal and informal education. Reading for pleasure is a means of educating yourself. Likewise, cultivating new loves in your life requires a choice and personal action.

Loss of love in any form is understandably a major fear for most people. Rather than dwell on that fear, work on creating the best possible relationships in the here and now that can provide good memories when loss does occur. Take each moment by moment and live in the now. This is the only time that you have, so do your very best to make the most of it.

Fourth Basic Fear—Fear of the Loss of Love

Dr. Napoleon Hill

The fourth basic fear, the fear of the loss of love, stems from the basic need for love which every human being has, and is aggravated by the tremendous competition that goes on in the selection of a mate. It is the fear upon which jealousy is based. It is probably the most dangerous of all fears for it sometimes leads to permanent mental unbalance. It can also be very costly. The important aspects of love were discussed in the section on motives. If you recall this discussion, you will realize that there is no reason why you should harbor this fear. The affectionate response between man and woman, which is the type of love one most fears losing, is one of the great blessings in this world, and it can be yours...very surely yours...if you pursue it with a positive mental attitude and are willing to pay its price. This holds true of the other forms of love which also are so very important to the individual, as, for example, the love of parents for children and children for parents.

Source: *PMA: Science of Success*, Educational Edition, Napoleon Hill Foundation, 1983; page 99.

Chapter 23

EMBRACE EVERY STAGE OF LIFE (FEAR OF OLD AGE)

*Are our thoughts so important? Well, our thoughts
become our words, our words become our actions, our
actions become our habits, and our habits become our
character. From thoughts to character, from thoughts
to biochemistry, from thoughts to health or disease,
the pathway is clear.*

—ARNOLD FOX, MD and BARRY FOX, PHD

Nearing old age is something each person will have to
deal with in their own manner as calendar age increases.
Growing old can result in pleasant circumstances if the latter
years are well-planned for in advance. Anticipating retirement
from everyday work but not retirement from everyday living
may be a good way to begin. Deciding to pursue new or
neglected hobbies, dedicating a portion of your week to
volunteer services, traveling, increasing family time, and
finding personal enrichment in reading, gardening, spiritual
development as well as simply resting are all ways we can fill
the time and be fulfilled as well.

Each stage of life can be a renewal and a rebirth for everyone if the new phase is not looked upon as a death knell, but rather a ringing-in of the new you. Dr. Hill reminds us frequently that we can make best use of our time if we budget it for balanced and optimal use. Too much rest and not enough activity can cause us to lose skills that may have taken a lifetime to acquire. Rather than give up something completely, why not scale back or chunk your time instead? For example, a lengthy job that might be accomplished in two eight-hour intervals may now be divided up over a time period of ten partial days with other activities interspersed. Plans can be flexible and adaptable now that time belongs more to you and less to others.

As you anticipate changes in your work schedule, why not look forward to things you have always wanted to do if time permits? Novels are waiting to be read, day trips or longer ones are waiting to be taken, recipes are simmering in cookbooks, and friends are looking to be asked to accompany you on your journey to better living. Start the list now, review it later, and live it as soon as you can. As the poet Robert Browning states:

> *Grow old along with me!*
> *The best is yet to be,*
> *The last of life, for which the first was made:*
> *Our times are in His hand*
> *Who saith "A whole I planned,*
> *Youth shows but half; trust God: see all, nor be afraid!"*

Fifth Basic Fear—Fear of Old Age

Dr. Napoleon Hill

Fear of old age is the fifth basic fear. We like to jump on this fear with both feet, and to laugh about it—because it is a lot better to laugh than to cry about it. When you have a birthday, take a year off your age instead of adding one. Thus you will begin to feel younger and to change in appearance so that you will look younger. This will be so because you will have sold yourself on the idea of youth rather than old age.

It has been discovered that some of the men of greatest achievement have done their life's best work after fifty-five, and some even after sixty and seventy. The reason for this is that nature compensates you for the loss of youth with one of the greatest things in the world—wisdom. Wisdom comes from experience, and experience comes with age. One has a good time when he or she is twenty, twenty-five and thirty, but when we have passed these years, we would not choose to go back to them again. We are more useful to the world as we mature. True enough, we can no longer stay up such long hours and get around so well at night, but most of these activities disappear with maturity.

Source: Adapted from *PMA: Science of Success,* Educational Edition, Napoleon Hill Foundation, 1983; pages 100-101.

Chapter 24

BOOK WORM BENEFITS
(FEAR OF LOSING LIBERTY)

*If you will read one book a year, you will actually be
above average. If you read one a month, you will enter
the top percentile. As too often happens to us human
beings, the easy access to books and information has
diminished their worth in our minds.*

—Jim Stovall

Recently I visited Monticello, the home of Thomas
Jefferson, located near Charlottesville, Virginia. I was not
only impressed with Jefferson's estate that included innovative
architecture and gardens, but also with the emphasis that he
placed on his library and personal correspondence. The only
conclusion one could reach from touring his home and listening
to the guides recant history was that President Jefferson,
author of the Declaration of Independence, took democracy
seriously and wanted to educate people as to the process that
would ensure liberty for them and for their descendants. The
self-evident truths that Mr. Jefferson related are not always self-
evident, or practiced, as we know from countries still having

civil and foreign conflicts. But these truths are the cornerstone for advanced civilizations.

Hear, hear, Mr. President!

Thomas Jefferson gathered his ideas from books. Books were among his dearest possessions, and so dear, in fact, that he used his personal library as the seedling for the Library of Congress. This one act indicated that Jefferson valued literacy and reading as habits to be cultivated. The center of his estate was his library and everything emanated from the one room lined with books.

If we fear the loss of liberty, then we can either be frozen in our tracks or do something about it. Lost liberty amounts to losing our collective soul as a nation. History only has to be reviewed to

comprehend what this means for a people, a nation, and a culture. Loss of liberty is unacceptable and can be circumvented through education, and education comes through reading.

Isn't it time that you read a good book that can support our country's collective wellness? Thomas Jefferson built our Declaration of Independence from wisdom he acquired in his area of reading. What will you create with your knowledge?

Sixth Basic Fear—Fear of the Loss of Liberty

Dr. Napoleon Hill

Fear of the loss of liberty, the sixth basic fear, is the opposite of the desire for freedom of body and mind, one of the basic motives previously discussed. And this fear is prevalent throughout the world today, for we know that certain influences are constantly and deliberately working to destroy the hard-won liberties so dear to humankind. People all around the world, in centuries past and in more recent years, have shed precious blood to gain and maintain the personal and political liberties which we now enjoy. They are not to be taken for granted or held lightly. A positive mental attitude demands that we make the most constructive use of our liberties and be ever vigilant in their defense.

One does not have to be a prophet, or possessed of any special perception, to discern the serious threats to our liberty which are daily gaining ground in the world. One of the basic ideas of the PMA Science of Success philosophy is that the American way of life, the democratic way of life, is essential to individual achievement on any level. Here is something worthy of your most serious thinking. We must be on the alert to preserve our liberties. Liberty is something clearly bought and preserved only by constant vigilance.

Source: *PMA: Science of Success,* Educational Edition, Napoleon Hill Foundation, 1983; pages 101-102.

Chapter 25

REMEMBERING THE GOOD
TIMES (FEAR OF DEATH)

*I have had much love in my life and I am very
fortunate. Without my grandfather's loving sacrifice,
I would not be here today, would not be writing
this. Of all the things that I have learned over the
years, the most important is the knowledge that love
is all that matters, and that, with love, all things are
possible.*

—Andrew Bienkowski

Many people believe that the opposite of fear is love.
Napoleon Hill states that the opposite of fear is faith.
He believes that you cannot be fearful if you are being faithful.
Still, the great granddaddy of all fears, the fear of death, can
come upon us and deliver a knockout punch that causes one
to reel for months, maybe years. Once a person stabilizes, the
overwhelming hurt recedes and the good memories begin to
surface and this is where love enters again. Remembering the
good times puts fear on the back burner and allows faith to
rekindle in our hearts.

Death hurts. No doubt about it. It makes no difference if it is someone else's or your own. But, belief in the positive nature of the universe, the overall goodness of God, and the expectation of something yet to come can be positive approaches to confronting this fear of fears. However you look at it, death is still one of the universe's greatest mysteries. It may just hold the greatest surprise package that lies in wait of our homecoming as well.

When our friends and family begin to transition, we look for signs from them that would indicate all is well after death. Recently, my sister passed away and I continue to talk to her in my mind. Last week, when I received some good news, a thought came to me, "I can't do things for you, but I can do things through you." I appreciate this message because it endorses Dr. Hill's concept that we must take immediate action to kick in the assistance of the Universe. My sister can only work through me now, but I can also aid in keeping her memory alive by acting in her behalf. Isn't life a wonderful, reciprocal process? The good that we do is the only thing that we can take with us at the end of life, and possibly the only thing we can give back.

Our guest columnist, Andy Bienkowski, discusses this concept in his wonderful book mentioned below. Many life lessons can be learned from his experiences. Consider reading it. It will make for a better understanding of the death and living process.

Seventh Basic Fear—Fear of Death

Dr. Napoleon Hill

The fear of death, the seventh and last basic fear, is the grandfather of them all. This one is always difficult to whip because of the complex background of the social inheritance of many people. This is really a very strong fear—and a universal one.

From the beginning of time, humankind has sought the answers to the questions, "Whence have I come?" and "Whither am I going?" There is a tendency to fear anything which we do not understand and for which we do not have complete, absolute answers. How can we overcome this fear?

Well, all the author can do is to tell you how he has succeeded in keeping this fear quieted within himself. He analyzed what we call life, and what we call death, by observing the way nature works. He found that there are only a few things in the entire universe which can be recognized and isolated. These are time and space, energy and matter, and back of them all: intelligence. These five things are all nature has to work with, and a study of elementary physics reveals that one can neither create nor destroy energy or matter. These two elements may be transformed from one form into the other, but they cannot be destroyed. Life is energy, if it is anything. If you cannot create or destroy energy, you can't destroy life; and nature doesn't destroy it either. That which we call life, like other forms of energy, may pass through successive changes or transitions, but it cannot be destroyed. Death, or the change we thus designate, is probably only a transition.

So the author said to himself: "Death is probably one of two things: either death is just one long eternal sleep, or else, if it isn't sleep, it's an experience on some plane far better than we have on this earth. In either event, there is nothing to fear because it's going to come anyway."

Source: *PMA: Science of Success,* Educational Edition, Napoleon Hill Foundation, 1983; pages 102-103.

Chapter 26

PERSONALITY POWER

"Your brain tumor has returned." It seems odd to me that such a simple, five-word sentence can have such a dramatic, lasting effect on so many lives. Over the past three years, without ever having studied the teachings of Dr. Napoleon Hill, my wife has been battling her brain tumor by employing many of the Seventeen Principles of Success without even knowing about it.

—DAN KUDULIS

When we understand the message of the Science of Success course created by Dr. Napoleon Hill, its immediate application in our lives becomes a matter of habit. Whether we are faced with adversity or experiencing positive results should not change our interpretation or activation of the principles. This success philosophy is not only useable when things are going our way, but more importantly part of life's program when things are spiraling out of control.

When this happens to me—either good or not so good results—I like to review the principles in short order and see which ones I am applying and which ones I am not. This works as a crosscheck to stabilize my behavior and either keeps me on track or puts me back on track.

To assist you in this process, artist Michael Telapary has created a collage of the seventeen original artworks that he has included in his book *Envisioning Success*. You can utilize this collage to remind you both consciously and subconsciously of the principles and do a quick check as to whether or not you are forming habits related to the outcomes you want in life. This quick check self-assessment tool is available as an interactive Flash movie available for both PC and Mac. If you find this tool helpful, you might also want to read Michael Telapary's book in full. I can highly recommend his approach to envisioning the principles for success in art and word.

If your aim is right, generally your outcome will be positive. Here's how to proceed:

- Daily review the Seventeen Success Principles using the beautifully illustrated collage.

- Click on each depiction, asking the questions that are aligned. Do this much as you would if you were conducting an examination of your behavior for good and/or bad results.

- Then self-correct your approach. This examination of conscience will help you stay on track, ultimately achieving the success you envision.

You can do it if you think you can.

What Do We Mean by Belief?

Dr. Napoleon Hill

"Wishing won't make it so," runs an old saying. This is true, and helps you remember a wish is not a belief.

A wish takes place, as it were, upon the surface of the mind. I wish…you may say, and follow with any wish that tickles your fancy…to have a million dollars drop into your lap…to be able to flap your arms and fly. A wish is not limited by natural forces. That very apparent fact, however, is not the main difference between a wish and a belief.

A belief is created, as it were, in the depths of the mind. A belief becomes part of you. That is why a true, deep belief can change your glandular secretions and the content of your bloodstream, and work other physical changes beyond the power of medical science to explain. Again, a belief, radiating its unknown wavelength from the depths of your mind to the depths of another mind, accounts for a good deal of "personality power" and much else on which we can put only the clumsiest of labels. It is belief in a cause—much stronger than a wish to stay alive—which causes people to transcend the instinct of self-preservation. It is belief that founds religion, sustains nations, stands behind anything great that ever is achieved.

A belief, I repeat, is part of you; that is why you can achieve what you believe. Moreover, when you hold a great belief, you believe all the time, just as, all the time, you go on living.

Source: *Grow Rich with Peace of Mind,* Ballantine Books, NY, August 1996; page 191.

Chapter 27

OPINIONS—CHEAPEST COMMODITY ON EARTH

As accurate thinkers, we must let no one do our thinking for us. We must establish standards by which to guide ourselves. However, sometimes our standards will give us a temporary disadvantage. In addition to painstaking labor to get the facts, sticking to our standards is the price we must pay as accurate thinkers.

—MARK FERGUSON

Accurate thinking means recognizing the difference between opinions and facts. Napoleon Hill states, "Opinions are the cheapest commodity on earth. Everybody has them." Facts, on the other hand, withstand scrutiny. Facts are researchable and time-tested. Opinions are capricious and resemble the chameleon that changes colors to blend in with its environment. By asking someone the simple question, "How do you know?" anyone can begin to discern fact from fiction.

Everyone is not credible although many people would like us to believe that they are. If you feel that you are being cheated, swindled, hoodwinked, misled, "taken for a ride," overwhelmed with information, or just plain bamboozled, you can fight back. You do not have to go along with what someone proposes unless you want to. If you are skeptical of the offer, stop in your tracks and say that you will do your own homework and get back to them. Next, begin to check things out for credibility and see if you can find support for anything that was said. Usually, when charlatans realize that you are not falling for the hype, they prey on another victim and leave you alone.

Knowing how to handle situations in the real world can save you precious time and money. If something appears too good to be true, it usually is. The test is simple. If you are promised something for nothing, it is almost certain that nothing of value is what you will receive. Hard work and effort are what produce positive outcomes and anything else is just a hook used to catch you unaware.

Do what works. Create success through the application of the Seventeen Success Principles. These time-tested and honored traits of those who have succeeded can serve you better than any handout or promise ever could. Reach for success, but remember to invest in your own ladder before you begin the climb. You are only as strong as you condition yourself to be. Success requires your best effort, and ultimately you will benefit the most from your training.

Fact Versus Fiction

Dr. Napoleon Hill

Gossips and scandalmongers are unreliable sources from whom to procure facts on any subject, although it is well known that they inspire much of the daily thinking of many people.

Wishes are often fathers to facts, as most people assume facts to harmonize with their wishes. Information based upon opinions and hearsay evidence is plentiful and most of it is free, but facts have an elusive habit, and generally there is a definite price attached to them—the price of painstaking labor in examining them for accuracy.

The favorite question of the accurate thinker is, "How do you know?" The thinker demands evidence of the soundness of information furnished. This person knows that many opinions are mere hopeful wishing, and not the result of careful analysis of facts.

The accurate thinker prays with faith because he or she has examined the evidence of the existence of a Creator as it is provided by the system and order of the universe, the harmony of all natural laws, and the relationship of time, energy, and matter as revealed, not by people's opinions, but by known facts uncovered by scientists. Thus we see that faith is a state of mind that can best be attained by the principles of accurate thinking based upon established facts. Understanding this, we can see the importance of adopting the habits of accurate thinking. Accurate thinkers know the fallacy of endeavoring to deceive others with loosely gathered opinions and makes it their business never to deceive themselves with such opinions.

Source: Adapted from *PMA: Science of Success,* Educational Edition, Napoleon Hill Foundation, 1983; pages 300-301.

Chapter 28

DEFINE PROBLEMS

Marriage is at its core a partnership where each partner agrees to take on certain responsibilities so that the partnership can thrive. Marriage does not mean that your spouse has the right to take the money which you earned before marriage or the inheritance which you received and appropriate half to themselves simply because they married you.

—ELIEZER ALPERSTEIN, CPA

Recently I saw a production of *The Wiz* at a local theater. One song that stayed in my mind was sung by Evillene, the Wicked Witch of the West, entitled, "No Bad News." The lyrics to this song are really commands to her subjects not to worsen her day by detailing any news that wasn't positive. Probably most of us can relate to this feeling and find ourselves desiring breaks from the media that seems, for the most part, only to deliver "bad news."

Looking at this from a different perspective, however, it is not so simple to remove ourselves from the equation. Sticking our heads in the sand, running for shelter, turning off the television, computer, radio, etc., simply does not undo the news.

We may receive a brief respite, yet the news is still the news and we are part of it in the making.

Do things in your immediate world escalate out of control? Do you help or hinder the process? If bills are unpaid and accounts are in arrears, is the world the culprit or are you also part of the problem? When we look within to understand what is happening in our external world, possibly we find that we have contributed to the making of the problem. Finger pointing is always easy, and a world wherein we are equipped with blinders not only shields us from the bad, but from the good we could envision as well.

Sometimes, exposing the problem and having society look at it dead-center saves us from beating around the bush. Knowing what we are dealing with is the very first step to solving any lingering problem. Define the problem, and then you can begin the process of creating a solution. Sweep a problem under the rug, and it will begin to grow until you finally wind up tripping over the bulge in the carpet. Why not diagnose the problem correctly from the onset, and recognize that suffering precedes healing? Both are essential in the cycle of life. With that said, let's *focus on the positive to eliminate the negative*. One can only exist because of the other.

Listen to that Still, Small Voice

Dr. Napoleon Hill

It is a known fact that a prolonged illness often forces one to stop, look, and listen. Thus we often learn to understand that still, small voice which speaks from within and causes us to take inventory of the factors which have led to defeat and failure in the past.

"A fever," said Emerson, "a mutilation, a cruel disappointment, a loss of wealth, a loss of friends, seems at the moment unpaid loss, and unpayable. But the sure years reveal the deep remedial force that underlies all facts. The death of a dear friend, spouse, brother, lover, which seemed nothing but privation somewhat later assumes the aspect of a guide or genius; for it commonly operates revolutions in our way of life, terminates an epoch of infancy or of youth which was waiting to be closed, breaks up a wonted occupation, or a household, or style of living, and allows the formation of new ones more friendly to the growth of character.

"It permits or constrains the formation of new acquaintances, and the reception of new influences that prove of first importance to the next years; and the man or woman who would have remained a sunny garden flower, with no room for its roots and too much sunshine for its head, by the falling of the walls and the neglect of the gardener is made the banyan of the forest, yielding shade and fruit to wide neighborhoods of man."

Source: *PMA: Science of Success,* Educational Edition, Napoleon Hill Foundation, 1983; pages 380-381.

Chapter 29

ACCEPT ASSISTANCE

The lingo today sends out strong signals and is representative of the thoughts that thereby pattern the lives of our youth today. Let us all concentrate on sending out a positive message to our youth, for they are our future, and let us be careful of our choice of words and how we conduct our lives, which will ultimately in the long run mold theirs.

—PETE DELORENZO

A mentor is a person who wishes to share "the secrets of the ages" with a special person who is deemed worthy. How does a person acquire the "status" of being worthy? That's for the mentor to decide—not the student. If you have been mentored by someone, consider yourself lucky because you are in that slim category of people who have attracted someone's attention.

Maybe you have been selected because of your work ethic, your willingness to go the extra mile, your persistence in getting things done, your determination not to quit when confronted with adversity, or your innate intelligence. Regardless of the reason, you have caught someone's attention and they want to pass on their wisdom and success tips to you. This is a unique opportunity if you decide to participate. This legacy of life's lessons cannot be assimilated by just anyone. As Napoleon Hill states, the individual must be ready to receive the information.

Mentorship predisposes you to the accumulated life experiences of someone who wants to pass on what they have learned for the sake of posterity. It's wisdom that money cannot buy, and therefore that makes it invaluable. Never dismiss someone's desire to mentor you by asking, "What could this person possibly have to teach me?" Sometimes, people are brought together because there is a recognition or similarity in life's purpose. You resonate with the person for some reason and you remind the mentor of who he or she once were and see you becoming.

If you have been selected, consider yourself special and follow these simple rules:

1. Listen, listen, listen. This is not a dialogue, but a monologue. You learn more when you listen.

2. Apply what you have received. Application is the glue that binds knowledge to result. You only get results by doing, not thinking.

3. Pass it on. What you receive, you are required to gift again. Never hoard your knowledge and experience. Share and duplicate for greater results.

4. Express gratitude for what you have received. Thankfulness returns to you one hundredfold. Be thankful.

These actions will jump-start your success journey. And remember to thank your mentor for showing you the hidden pathway!

The Appropriate Use of Words

Dr. Napoleon Hill

The ability to speak in words and to enunciate clearly is a blessing which the Creator has bestowed on humans alone. No other living creature can speak. This is a blessing which should be highly prized and respected.

The English language, as well as the organized languages of other peoples and nations, is replete with words which carry every conceivable shade of meaning. It is possible to choose the right words: words which will attract and not repel. There is no excuse for the careless use of words which will offend the sensibilities of others.

The use of profanity, at any time or under any circumstances, is wholly inexcusable. Let us remember that when we use words of profanity, we profane the name of the Creator who endowed us with the ability to use words—an ability which should be used gratefully, to the greater glory of the Creator and edification of others.

The appropriate use of words is regarded as a sign of education and culture. The person who is able to use the proper words at the proper time has developed a very important factor in the achievement of a pleasing personality. While the inappropriate use of words can repel, the appropriate use of words, together with a pleasing and motivating tone of voice and pleasant facial expression, can go a long way toward gaining for one the attention, respect, confidence, and liking of other persons.

Source: *PMA: Science of Success,* Educational Edition, Napoleon Hill Foundation, 1983; pages 179-180.

Chapter 30

POSITIVE PURPOSE

Experience and knowledge are learned, accumulated over time, and may not be recognized immediately. A strong work ethic and the burning desire to succeed are not things that are taught or learned—they are characteristics that come from within. And they are noticed immediately. You don't have to put in years before someone notices hard work.

—Jeffrey Gitomer

To become our best, we must emulate those who have succeeded in achieving what it is we want to do. This sounds simple and easy enough to accomplish, but even though the evidence is plainly before us, many people fail to acknowledge what works. This is why individuals not only stumble through their own success initiatives, but also why entire programs do not reach the level of success that they aspire to reach.

Simply asking the question, "What's in it for me?" is insufficient. The better question to ask is, "How will I contribute today to make the world a better place in which to live?" Don't try to save the planet overnight, just make something that you touch a little better because you have seen a need and filled it.

Jeffrey Gitomer was our guest ezine columnist, and I have met Jeffrey on several occasions. I know that he not only writes, speaks, and markets his materials, he also helps others achieve their dreams. For example, this book is a compilation of articles in our ezine that is formatted and emailed weekly from Jeffrey Gitomer's office on a secure database. Several years ago he learned that the Napoleon Hill Foundation had a need for this service, and he had the capacity to offer it to us as a service—free of charge! So, for several years we have been thanking Jeffrey Gitomer for providing the Foundation with the delivery mechanism to make it happen. And we appreciate the opportunity that Jeffrey has provided us with weekly. Thanks, Jeffrey, for making our world a better place because of your service to us!

In being the very best person you can become, you must add in the elements of service and gratitude. Be of service whenever you are able and also remember to give daily thanks for the personal gifts that you have received. This two-step process will aid you in dedicating your life to a mission that has a meaningful purpose and positive outcome. By being the very best you can be, you set the pace for others to follow. Follow true leaders who already have traveled the course.

A Philosopher's Creed

Dr. Napoleon Hill

Let me be open-minded on all subjects so that I may grow mentally and spiritually.

May the time never come when I will be above learning from the humblest person.

Let me never forget that a closed mind is a narrow mind.

May I never express opinions on any subject unless they are founded upon reasonable, dependable knowledge.

Forbid that I should ever find fault with another because he or she may not agree with me.

May I always show a wholesome respect for those with whom I may not agree.

Let me be always mindful of the fact that all my knowledge is as nothing when compared to all that remains to be learned.

Give me the courage to admit my ignorance when I am asked a question about which I know little or nothing.

May I always share with others such knowledge as I may possess which can be of help to them.

Let me never forget that humility of heart will attract more friends than all the wisdom of humankind.

Let me remain ever a student in search of truth, and never pretend to be a finished scholar on any subject.

Source: *PMA: Science of Success,* Educational Edition, Napoleon Hill Foundation, 1983; page 176.

Chapter 31

IMPROVEMENT, NOT PERFECTION

Without a healthy being and without preserving ourselves properly, we do not have the means to think and grow rich. Pills, surgeries, and organ replacements are not the answer for our health and self-preservation because they are only temporary fixes at the best. The secret of achieving long-lasting, sound physical health lies in Dr. Hill's teaching and the faithful application of his teaching.

—PING YANG

It is never too late to focus on the picture-perfect end result. Knowing that you can improve your life by making one positive choice at a time points you in the right direction. Also, this power to choose allows you to begin stepping into the footsteps successful people have left behind as a trail for you to follow. By knowing that you do not have to do it all on a moment's notice, you establish a purpose and a plan for your journey. As you begin, the Universe locks onto your determination to succeed and you begin to lead the life you envision.

Really, success can begin with this simple start, but it also takes discipline and much perseverance to advance to the higher levels. For starters, here are some tips to follow:

- Begin each day anew. Forget the setbacks and focus on comebacks.

- Lighten your journey. Leave yesterday in the past and embrace your future.

- Take time to refresh your mind, body, and spirit as you transition to an improved you.

- Reward yourself when you accomplish daily goals. It's good to feel good.

- Extend a helping hand to others by sharing the goodness you possess. Joys shared are not halved, but doubled.

- Chronicle your progress by keeping a daily log. Record positive actions and review at the end of the day. By counting your positive actions, you soothe yourself more than by counting sheep.

- Ask yourself if you made a positive difference in your life, someone else's life, or in the world today. If not, why not?

- Resolve to not defer or neglect to commit a good deed daily because you will never get the opportunity to repeat this day's performance.

- Focus on improvement not perfection.

- Address the entire you—spiritual, emotional, physical, mental, financial, and social—each day. Look at these elements of who you are as spokes on a wheel that need to be in balance. When balanced, you will roll comfortably on to your ultimate success destination.

It has been said that "What we think about we bring about." Focus on daily improvement, and not only will you feel better, but you will perform better too. The ultimate choice is yours. And, if one of the ten motives for voluntary action is self-preservation, then you'd better be about preserving the best you that you can create, one positive action at a time.

Do You Really Want
Professional Advice?

Dr. Napoleon Hill

Suppose some great man were to hand you an exquisite, beautifully built machine equipped with many self-repairing features. Suppose he explained to you that with reasonable care and proper handling, this machine would automatically, after about eighteen years of warming up, begin to deliver money from a slot, each week, in gradually increasing amounts for the next forty to sixty years. That the total amount delivered by this machine would not be less than two hundred thousand dollars. He might go on to say that if you really learned how to run and care for the machine like an expert, you might increase its output by millions of dollars.

Suppose the builder of this machine let you in on a little secret. He told you that there was another slot which every moment of its life produced either happiness and satisfaction, or despair and dejection. If you would learn to manipulate the controls for this slot with the deftness of an expert, the machine would purr at great speed, producing endless satisfaction and financial reward. He might warn you that it would take much patient learning and long trial and the careful following of instructions to achieve this result.

His parting words might be, "Others have done it before you, and there may be many who follow you. They all had one secret in common—they had faith in the machine and faith in me and faith in my instructions." With that, he might leave you to your own devices.

Now suppose that after many years of trial you had only half-mastered the technique and you learned that there were other experts who could help you. True, they had mastered only small segments of the knowledge of the master who built the machine; but if each in his field could help straighten you out and thus improve the way you handle your controls and the results you achieve, would you seek their advice?

Source: *PMA: Science of Success,* Educational Edition, Napoleon Hill Foundation, 1983; pages 451-452.

Chapter 32

TAKE CARE OF YOURSELF

Of the ten basic motives that inspire all human action, love is probably the most powerful. More has been accomplished by people motivated by love for mothers, fathers, wives, husbands and children than any of the other motives.

—Tom Cunningham

One of the primary motives for all action is love! It is the force that engages people and causes them to take immediate command of their time and talents. When we love individuals, family, friends, causes, etc., we are almost compelled to do whatever it takes to make dreams come true. All this talk about love causes one to wonder why we then put self-love on the back burner and allow the other "loves" of our lives to take precedence over our own?

I would like to suggest that if we care for ourselves first, we then have a wellspring from which to draw in the care of others. By denying ourselves the common goodwill we extend to others, we are depleting ourselves and on our way to a personal meltdown. Take time to care for yourself, and in doing so you will be better equipped to care for others.

In caring for yourself, have you done the following lately?

1. Taken a holiday of your own choosing?

2. Declined work when you were already overloaded?

3. Asked someone for help instead of shouldering the work on your own?

4. Granted yourself personal quiet time instead of filling every minute of each day with a time-synchronized to-do list?

5. Turned down a request for a lunch date, get-together, or friend's night out just because you would rather do something else?

6. Read a book, watched a show, listened to a CD, taken a walk, shopped where you wanted to, and eaten what you wanted because it pleased you?

7. Created a day with your own agenda from morning to night?

8. Said "no" without feeling guilty or second-guessing your motives?

9. Considered what makes you happy?

10. Planned for the future instead of dreading it?

If we give ourselves more to enjoy, we will be healthier, happier, and more terrific than we can even imagine. You have heard the financial concept of paying yourself first, right? Well, look to this day for you first, and do what it is that brings joy to your life. From this perspective, all things look more positive and appealing.

The Chemistry of Love

Dr. Napoleon Hill

Recognize that love and affection constitute the finest medicines for both your body and your soul. Love changes the entire chemistry of the body and conditions it for the expression of a positive mental attitude. And love also extends the space you may occupy in the hearts of others. And in this connection, it is important to remember that while love is free, the best way to receive it is to give it.

Keep a daily diary of your good deeds in behalf of others, and never let the sun set on a single day without recording some act of human kindness. The benefits of this habit will be cumulative and eventually it will give you domain over great spaces in the hearts of others. And remember: One good deed each day will keep old man gloom away.

For every favor or benefit you receive, give an equal benefit to others. The law of increasing returns will operate in your favor and eventually...perhaps very soon...it will give you the capacity to get everything you are entitled to receive. A positive mental attitude must have a two-way highway on which to travel, or it will cease to function.

Source: *PMA: Science of Success,* Educational Edition, Napoleon Hill Foundation, 1983; pages 228-229.

Chapter 33

FAITHFUL VERSUS FEARFUL

I started asking myself what I needed to do to change the outcome and turn this negative situation into something better than positive—something simply amazing. I was on my way because I had eliminated feeling fearful and stopped all the negative talk. I began to formulate a masterful plan. It was so simple; how could I have let myself fall so hard?

—RAVEN BLAIR DAVIS

Are the fears that are holding you back real or are they figments of your imagination? If you are brutally honest with yourself, you will admit that most often the details that you worry about are created in your daydreams. As we "worry," we begin to spin a mental yarn that escalates out of control until we manage to frighten even ourselves. As we storyboard fear, we can cause ourselves to be frozen in our tracks.

Sometimes we can even witness family or friends using this tactic on themselves. A story is created and "what ifs" are added and before you know it fear rears its head in monstrous fashion. Literally, a person can arouse fear just by thinking intensely about it. Our minds have great powers; and when we use our power of visualization to create what we want to avoid, we actually are allowing those negative mental pictures to come closer and closer to our reality.

When we recognize this negative tendency, can we reverse the downward spiral? Absolutely! Simply catch yourself being negative and say silently or out loud, "Stop it!" Then, replace that negative thought with something good that may as easily happen. For example, a person may be fearful about an upcoming meeting or work situation. Instead of envisioning the worst that might happen, shift gears and imagine the best possible outcome and even make a game of it. When you trick yourself into thinking positively, you will realize that by thinking negatively you were being the butt of your own joke. Fear causes us to act fearfully, and fearful actions usually produce fearful results.

Just for today, give up a negative addiction. Catch yourself being negative in your thought process. Refuse to indulge in fear-based thoughts. Stop negative thoughts before they filter into your reality. Be faithful instead of fearful, and in a very short time you will see a change in not only your worldview but your world.

Replace Fear with Faith

Dr. Napoleon Hill

The first problem we have is to replace fear with understanding and faith in ourselves. To do this, let us examine the mechanism of fear and its relation to bodily function.

First and foremost, let me tell you that temporary, fleeting fear is a very important and quite normal function of the human mind. The fleeting fear of being hit as we cross the street only serves to make us cautious—it protects our life—by momentarily forcing our attention on the problem of getting across safely. Thus, fear teaches us caution, but the fear is forgotten as soon as we have safely crossed.

The second important purpose of fear is to mobilize the body functions in defense of our life against a threatening situation. Consider for a moment early primitive man, sitting, warmed by his fire in the gathering dusk, and enjoying a meal prepared during the day. Certainly, this early man was at peace with the world, and the toils of the day were forgotten. At this moment let us say, a twig cracked in the forest—a sign of danger. An enemy was near.

Frequently fear is no longer a reaction to a specific danger, but a thoroughly learned habit of response, perhaps learned in early childhood. Although the need of this response has long since been lost, the pattern of thinking may persist, and now is defeating your quest for happiness and effective living. We fear most the unknown. Seek knowledge and understanding of your fear, and it will be replaced by faith. One must cultivate and nurture a positive mental attitude to achieve that smooth, effectively functioning mind-body you are seeking.

Source: *PMA: Science of Success,* Educational Edition, Napoleon Hill Foundation, 1983; pages 428-430.

Chapter 34

THE ENERGY OF EMOTION

Lots of people claim to be atheists. Whenever I meet them I like to ask them to tell me about the God they don't believe in, because I probably don't believe in their God either.

—FR. ROBERT SIPE

Energy is the invisible fuel in our bodies that enables us to carry out the daily duties, processes and functions that result from our desires. It is stated that energy cannot be destroyed; however its form can be changed in order to achieve certain end results. Being positively minded, we should always be about achieving the picture-perfect end result for whatever it is we are striving to achieve. It is energy that causes the seed to sprout, the flower to blossom, and the faded blooms to return to the soil to initiate the process all over again. Energy surrounds us and is embedded within us, but the purpose of energy and its application is determined by us through the use of our free will.

Our time is limited by design, and what projects we undertake in this lifetime require us to calculate how we will use our talents and gifts wisely. If we are to put concrete foundations under our castles in the sky, then we must begin to locate the cement, activate a cement mixer, and get the entire process underway—otherwise our castles remain figments of our imaginations, sons and daughters of our daydreams.

Getting to the point, we must direct our limited energies to what we want to achieve and not dissipate them on things of no consequence. Time can be wasted in years, months, days or even seconds, and before long the sands in the hourglass have run out and we have nothing to show for the time we were given. Repetitive actions can only achieve the same results, so select actions that are worthy of your dedication of time, your most precious commodity.

By focusing on what we want to achieve or do that will create a lasting impact, we are directing our energies to what is truly important to us. First you acquire the dream, and then you work to bring that dream to reality through transmuting or directing otherwise wayward energies to the accomplishment of daily goals that enable you to move forward. You can't do this by whittling away your hours in bed, in front of the TV, socializing, or just dealing with life with a devil-may-care attitude. To achieve greatness, you must be ready to focus, specialize, and deliver the goods on a schedule that you create and master every single day.

Nothing is more valuable than our time; and when that runs out, all the wishing in the world won't bring back even a second more of living. So spend your time wisely, use it to express your personal talent on this planet, and leave a visible, lasting legacy for others to follow, that will ensure your energies were well-used and well-spent. Our goal in the end, to paraphrase Erma Bombeck, is to return to our Creator with every single talent and gift given at birth entirely used up and ready to be refilled with the Spirit from which we came.

Sex and Sublimation

Dr. Napoleon Hill

Of all the gifts humankind has been given by the Creator, sex is at once the most precious, constructive drive and also the most debased. Sex is behind all the creative forces that work to advance us toward human destiny. It has built our great cathedrals and institutions of learning. It was responsible for the creation of this democracy to give the children of the future rights and freedom that our forefathers never knew. The sublimation of it gave us the Leonardo da Vincis, the Michelangelos, and the Darwins, Beethovens, and multitudes of people of history who stand like giants on the road to eternity. It gave us our mother's undying love—the love that taught us how to love others. From it has sprung sympathy, kindness and understanding of others, and in its highest sense it has even taught us how to love Him better.

If we really put as much effort into our marriage as we do into our business problems, it will afford us some of the keenest moments of both physical and spiritual satisfaction. One can feel only the deepest sorrow for the few who have learned to debase marriage into vulgarity. They have missed one of the most exquisitely fine and delicately beautiful joys of life. And for those who have been unable to find satisfaction and joy in marital relationships, there is always available the help of the doctor.

Sex drive is a completely natural desire. What is more, it is among the more inspiring and action-producing desires. When driven by this desire, people develop keenness of the imagination, courage, ingenuity in the creation of ways and means to attain definite ends, persistence, and creative ability unknown to them from other sources of inspiration.

When the desire is harnessed and directed to the attainment of definite ends, it often lifts people to heights of achievement which give them the reputation of being geniuses. The emotion of sex contains the secret of great creative ability and creative vision.

Source: Adapted from *PMA: Science of Success,* Educational Edition, Napoleon Hill Foundation, 1983; pages 450-451.

Chapter 35

LIFE AFTER DEATH

There is an ancient tomb structure in Ireland called Newgrange. It was constructed with a strategic opening that lets a beam of sunshine enter the innermost dark chambers at the rising of the winter solstice sun. This was the expression of Neolithic man's innate desire for life after death. Not much has changed with post-modern man today. Although we have advanced with our greater technology, the questions and mystery of life and death remain.

—URIEL MARTINEZ

Due to being out of the country I did not hear about the deaths of two good friends until I returned. Both of their services had occurred and all that remained were the memories that I shared with each of these remarkable people. Reflecting on the days we spent together causes me to wonder exactly what happens with the gifts and talents these people possessed. Both of these friends were teachers, and over the years I had the opportunity to work with them in and out of the classroom. As friends and family transition, it is only natural that those left behind begin to consider their own mortality.

I have heard people say, "If I die" when talking about their physical existence. It is natural to desire to live forever; however, human bodies are not designed for eternity in their current form. But what about our spirits? Isn't there a time-lessness to our dreams and desires that possess an eternity all their own? I like to believe that our spiritual personalities grow more beautiful as we age and that this is the aspect of ourselves that we truly cultivate and make more attractive as our physical selves decline. Instead of facelifts, crowns, hair coloring, and bodybuilding, we can beautify our spiritual selves by giving away our intangible gifts received upon birth.

Have you gifted the world with your own special talents, or are they still lingering inside you? One way to become immortal is to continue to exist in the hearts and minds of those people you have served in your lifetime. Whether you write a poem, short story, novel, play, or create an artwork, people can still see the visible efforts of your talents put to use after you are no longer here. By extending a helping hand, listening when a person needs to talk, offering advice that is useful and practical, and focusing on another's needs first, you are able to add beauty to your inner spirit. From this wellspring of invisible gifts, your inner self begins to outgrow your body, and it is time to go back home and align with its original source.

I wonder what change awaits each and every one of us when we die? When the egg hatches and a chick emerges, when the caterpillar awakens as a butterfly, when the acorn germinates to become the oak, and when the newborn looks around and sees the world for the first time, isn't there something even more remarkable we can anticipate in our transition? Literally, "See you at the top" can take on a whole different meaning. So as Dr. Hill reminds us, our desire for life after death has been placed in us at our conception. It is innate. And it is faith in this gift that will enable us to spend our lives in the present moment to the fullest, and next journey onward to an even greater future in the spirit. Life must be lived in context of the present moment, and it is good to always remember that there is only the present moment. Therefore, life does go on.

The Desire for Life after Death

Dr. Napoleon Hill

The desire for life after death. This is a very strong motive and it is the one upon which nearly all religious activity is based. Surveys have been made of the peoples of the world and they show that every culture, from the lowest degree of social development to the highest, worships something. They all have some form of religion. And, oddly enough, the central theme of all such religions is immortality, or everlasting life. Some students of this subject have suggested that perhaps the greatest evidence favoring a belief in the continuation of consciousness after earth life, lies in the persistence with which this idea recurs in all cultures. A desire for perpetual life is closely allied with the desire for self-preservation and it is instinctive in the nature of humanity.

Source: *PMA: Science of Success,* Educational Edition, Napoleon Hill Foundation, 1983; pages 20-21.

Chapter 36

FREEDOM—AN EARNED PRIVILEGE

True freedom is to see the body and the mind as one. Our mind cannot feel calm if our body is out of balance, and vice versa. Often the body and the mind are at odds with each other, and for many of us, this is the root of our suffering.

—Rev. Dr. Sam Boys

Examining the concept of freedom causes us to first consider what enslaves a person. One definition of enslavement is one person being "owned" by another. This loss of personal freedom still exists today; however, a more common form is the power of enslavement that we ourselves provide to objects that reign over us in our homes and at work. The care and feeding of possessions can cause them to own us rather than vice versa. Consider whether the objects you own service you or enslave you, and you will begin to comprehend that the individuals who are the most free understand how accumulating possessions can put them in a caregiver's role.

As mentioned in a previous chapter, custodians are people put in charge of something that they look after. Whether a child, building, financial securities, or collection of some type, custodians are accountable for their charge. Over the years, collections accumulate and the joy in acquiring can quickly turn into the task of caregiving. Somewhere in the transition, the freedom of body and mind are abdicated for a choice freely made.

The things that bind us control us. Through choices made, a person exchanges one opportunity for another. To be free really means to be in control of choices and their outcomes. Collecting can lead to hoarding. Movement relieves stagnation, and circulation keeps the life blood flowing in our bodies. Energy that is circulated empowers. Movement relieves inertia. Life improves with positive choices made that are selective and predispose us to good outcomes.

So in order to be free in body and mind, it is necessary to freely make and execute good choices—one at a time. These baby steps toward self-actualization lead us to more empowered end results. Knowing what to do and then doing it heightens our awareness about the freedoms we can and do control. Freedom is not a "given," rather it is a "right" that we earn one positive choice at a time. Membership in a free society is not an entitlement but rather an earned privilege. If you have this "golden" opportunity, remember to not leave home without it! Circulate the idea and empower yourself and those around you. True freedom comes with accountability to both you and others. Let it motivate you to become the person you envision.

Hill exclaims, "If you have the power to advance…if you are certain that you can have a better future, you'll never surrender your birthright of freedom."

The Desire for Freedom of Body and Mind

Dr. Napoleon Hill

The desire for freedom of body and mind. The basic wish in everyone's heart is the desire to be free and unfettered. Ask average people you meet and they will tell you that someday "I'm going to be my own boss and nobody is going to tell me what to do." This elementary expression of a basic urge does not go beyond a mere idle wish in most cases, and sometimes it is just plain laziness that prompts it, rather than a definite desire to be free. In fact, working for oneself does not necessarily mean freedom. There are men and women who own their own businesses who work early and late to make ends meet while their employees work their eight hours and go home. But these are unusual situations. It is true that owning your own business is one way to be self-determining.

This great country of ours affords more opportunities for personal freedom than anywhere else in the world. It is up to the individual to take advantage of the opportunity by having a definite idea of what he or she wants which will create freedom, and a definite plan by which to obtain individual purpose. Freedom of body and mind requires very careful planning to achieve and "few there be that find it." Many persons, even with money, bind themselves to too many things and fail to be really free.

As long as you are willing to let life push you around, it will.

Source: Adapted from *PMA: Science of Success,* Educational Edition, Napoleon Hill Foundation, 1983; page 21.

Chapter 37

SELF-SABOTAGE

If there is one emotion that is completely void of the essential quality of good sense, tolerance, accurate thought and wisdom, it is that emotion we call revenge. It quickly derails one from his definite chief aim, causes a loss of focus, drains one's vital positive energy, and ultimately self-sabotages one's own journey toward achievement.

—PHIL TAYLOR

Instead of focusing on revenge when the motive overtakes you, why not focus on a blessing? Everyone can bless someone or something as a way of acknowledging their exposure to what they experienced or what they witnessed first or secondhand. Acknowledge the affront, bless it and the perpetrator, and then let it go! As you throw out the garbage, you will feel the grace of the decision made in your behalf.

If you see something that is good, bad, or in-between that catches your attention, bless it and move forward. Revenge gets you caught in the track of retaliation, one-upmanship, and is always a train wreck about to happen. Why go there? Better to release the hurt that produced the desire to hurt back in the first place. End the vicious cycle before it gets started. You can do it.

When we feel crossed or wronged, the desire for revenge pushes our rational capacity into the background. Emotion rules and heads roll. In the end, however, both parties are harmed. The one who causes the situation and the one who responds to it in an aggressive, vengeance-seeking way are both injured.

In responding to getting even in a positive way, you are not ignoring the wrong or negating the wrong. Rather you are dissolving the control that it has over you. Try this and see if it works for you. When it does, and it will, you can then focus on polishing your positive motives for success and you will arrive at your destination in record time.

The Desire for Revenge

Dr. Napoleon Hill

Although the feeling of getting even with someone is basically human, it is utterly wasteful. It builds or improves nothing—and no one. Holding a grudge can result in only one thing—a negative mental attitude, which is exactly opposite to the constructive or positive mental attitude which is required for success. Getting angry and holding hatred in our hearts is a waste of mental energy, a dissipation of our psychic force and an unproductive use of our precious time. You would be astounded, however, to know how much energy some people put into the desire for revenge—and the desire to strike back. "I'll take it out of his pockets or hang his hide on the barn door." How often have you heard that or its equivalent?

Source: *PMA: Science of Success,* Educational Edition, Napoleon Hill Foundation, 1983; pages 21-22.

Chapter 38

HATE—A ROBBER BARON

The emotion of hate is not like an arrow, but is in fact like a boomerang, which if aimed at others with an intent to harm, will ultimately only come back more forcefully to the person who launches it.

—ADIL DALAL

Hate is truly a double-edged sword because it can wound our creativity and cause us to become frozen in our tracks toward success. It can become a perpetual detour or roadblock that forces us into a standstill and handcuffs us emotionally. Hate is as much a disservice to ourselves as to anyone we direct the hate toward. The emotionally charged actions ricochet back to both the doer and receiver of the hateful intention and keep the cycle going. Hate has no ending other than negativity. In this regard, two negatives do not equal a positive.

The art of turning the other cheek is not for the benefit of the perpetrator, but for the benefit of the person being wronged. By removing yourself from the equation, you refuse to take part in the negativity that can quickly grow out of control. As you stand back, gain perspective, and refuse to participate, you capture the upper hand in an emotionally charged confrontation.

Transforming hate into love is probably the hardest thing to do in this world. It's like turning base metal into gold. Alchemy of the spirit can transform each one of us from our lowest to our highest self just by the realignment of our thoughts, feelings, and emotions. But it is worth the ultimate effort. See what happens when you decide that revenge, hate, and retaliation are not worth your investment of time. Focus on what really counts and begin to put your best foot forward. When you look back at your life, have an album of lifetime achievements to remember rather than an album of regrets. Make the most of what you are given. Dr. Hill reminds us, "The only people you should get even with are those who have helped you."

Who to Get Even With!

Dr. Napoleon Hill

Revenge is a motive for action and a very strong one. It might be compared to racing the motor of your automobile while it is not in gear. The power developed is wasted: the fuel has been consumed, the energy expended, the machine worn, and still the car has not arrived anywhere. Such is the waste of energy and personal power when we harbor revenge in our minds and hearts. Also, you may be sure that it will kick back on anyone who permits this desire to remain. Newton states in one of his laws: To every action there is an equal amount of reaction. This law, which pertains to the physical properties of matter, is also applicable to the eighth motive, the desire for revenge, with a slight alteration: There will be an equal and opposite force resulting from the expression of revenge. The only people you should get even with are those who have helped you.

The more commonly expressed negative emotions, and the more dangerous, are: fear, hate, anger, jealousy, revenge, vanity, and greed. These are the seven robber barons which often deprive people of their opportunity of achievement because they make accurate thinking impossible. They should be under constant control and always subject to the closest scrutiny, for they lead to errors of judgment.

Source: *PMA: Science of Success,* Educational Edition, Napoleon Hill Foundation, 1983; pages 22, 302.

Chapter 39

YOUR ULTIMATE PURPOSE

Young children have the natural ability to express themselves and not worry too much about what others think. They aren't tainted by the pressures that develop as they begin to deal with peer pressure and develop a fear of failure. So consequently, they have the tendency to be themselves, and feel good about it.
—PHIL BARLOW

What does self-actualization mean? Supposedly it is the highest level of personal achievement wherein we do what it is we were put on this planet to accomplish. At different times in our lives it is different things, but sometimes there are these two or three haunting desires that do not leave us alone no matter our age. That little nudge, or that little idea that wakes us up at night, could just be the one thing that the Creator wants us to accomplish while on this side of heaven.

Let me tell you something about myself that few know—all of my life I have had a love affair with cats. From the cradle and probably to the grave, cats have ranked in the "very important" category to me. Currently, I have one special cat named Mole, (pronounced Moley—as in Guacamole), who is one of my all-time favorites. There have been others, but he is the one on this side of the rainbow, as I have heard others express it. By that I mean he is older, but hasn't transitioned yet. Recently, I traveled on a vacation to Alaska and was gone for several days. Although Mole was cat-sat at home, he still was glad to see me. Dr. Arcy, one of my traveling buddies, commented that "He actually smiled when he saw you." Not only did he do that, but he purred nonstop by my side for the entire night. What a welcome home greeting.

Now, what's the point of all this? The point is—back to self-expression—I have been haunted about doing something with and for cats for years. But, what to do and how to do it?

Long story short. A few years back, I met Michael Telapary from the Netherlands and he listened to my crazy cat ideas and thought that they were interesting. He helped me combine his musical talent with my cats' "purrforming" and together we launched a website dedicated to my family of feline friends. Is my life complete because I have done this? Well, I hope not, but it sparked my creativity, it aligned me with a friend who shares my passion, and it has allowed me to scratch another item off my Bucket List!

Crazy cat lady! Maybe. But let me ask you, what have you done with your passion? Is it still inside you? At least I have very tangible proof now that I have manifested something that I have only wished for in the past. And maybe, just maybe, it will make the world a better place, one purr at a time.

Self-Expression and Recognition

Dr. Napoleon Hill

We should be working harder for the opportunity to express ourselves and to gain public recognition than for any amount of money. There are a great many people who are doing just that and they become successful. Many thinking people believe that the ultimate purpose of all life is seeking new and better ways to express one's self. In the process by which life evolves new models it proceeds from a simple type of idea to a more complex one, for the reason that it wishes to enjoy a greater variety of impression and expression. The ego, the self-existent, living entity of humans, follows this principle and has this desire for expression. A rich source of satisfaction of this desire may be found in daily contacts with people, if contacts are made with a positive mental attitude.

In the business of becoming successful, you will find you will need both hands. One hand will be stretched upward, to receive the blessing of Infinite Intelligence, with the other extended down and outward, sharing and giving to others who are helping you in the climb. No one ever achieved outstanding success without the cooperation of others; and you realize, of course, that you must give something in return for this cooperation.

Source: *PMA: Science of Success,* Educational Edition, Napoleon Hill Foundation, 1983; pages 22, 24.

Chapter 40

DEMAND LIFE'S BEST

Value creation happens when a person makes a volitional decision to produce a product or service to fill a specific market need. Value is created by a person's ability to think. The time we spend thinking and acting is limited. We exchange our limited time to create value. Therefore we can equate value creation and work with our time here on earth.

—RAY STENDALL

Whenever I needed money and asked my mother for it, she always reminded me that "Money doesn't grow on trees, you know!" Thinking about this admonition now makes me smile because in an indirect way, my mother was preparing me to face my own future and learn about the science of getting rich. As I discussed career options with my children, I also told them that after four years of higher education I wanted them to be able to earn a living at their chosen profession. At the time I reminded them about the sources of income, they too smiled and thought that I didn't understand much.

Upon their graduation, both my son and daughter were employed full time in the area of their degrees. They now better understand that they need to harvest their living from their profession, not from handouts, loans, or the generosity of others.

Self-sufficiency leads to better self-esteem and a higher quality of life. Career counselors often talk about interests, talents, and the predisposition for certain professions—but do they talk enough about potential income? Sometimes students need to be reminded that they have to do something with the education they have acquired and not just accumulate knowledge within themselves. Like money, possessions, or anything else, things are only of value when they are in circulation.

Napoleon Hill states, "True happiness consists not in the possession of things, but in the privilege of self-expression through the use of material things." Ponder this thought a bit and see if you don't agree that things of value are really transferable energy that can be used to make our lives better. Movement creates a certain dynamic that keeps us on our toes. Money may not always grow on trees, but for those who own orchards, the apples translate into income. Likewise, whatever we devote our time and energy to, we should be expectant of equal compensation in whatever form we choose.

Demand Life's Best

Dr. Napoleon Hill

Criticism has been leveled by some people because they feel there is too much consideration for the material things in life. If we seem to overemphasize the importance of money and material riches, it is because so many people let fear of poverty ruin their chances to enjoy the other riches in life. The real good there is in money consists of the use to which it is put and not the mere possession of it. True happiness consists not in the possession of things, but in the privilege of self-expression through the use of material things. They are but a means to an end—physical instruments of impression and expression. You must have money in order to enjoy freedom of body and mind, which is a choice blessing. A person cannot be really free if he or she must be chained to a routine job most of the person's waking hours and receive in return for that a mere subsistence. If a person has to pay that much for existence, it is too high a price! These lessons will give you the formula for breaking with past habits of accepting the crumbs from life's table, and teach you a proven way in which you can rid yourself of self-imposed limitations and enjoy your fill of life's riches.

But let anyone who imagines that they do not want money try to get along without it. They will soon find out that one of the worst crimes a person can be guilty of is to be poverty-stricken and broke. Let us be realistic enough to face the facts of life and demand from life the best that it can give.

Source: Adapted from *PMA: Science of Success,* Educational Edition, Napoleon Hill Foundation, 1983; pages 24-25.

Chapter 41

EXPECT CHANGE

It's a widely accepted axiom that you can't change people. While it may be true that we can't, what we can control is our choice of the people we will surround ourselves with. There's no doubt we're in better stead to succeed and to contribute to the better good of all, when we dissociate from negative influences and connect ourselves deliberately with others who share our values and support each other's goals.

—KATHLEEN BETTS

When leaves change colors, when pears and apples ripen, when the sky darkens earlier and evening air has a crisp scent, we know that the season of fall is here. Houseplants are taken indoors and seasonal plants succumb to the frost. Many animals look for warmer lairs and some birds migrate south. Lawn furniture is stored, mowers are put away and the last of the summer garden is harvested. With all this occurring around us, there is little doubt that a season of change is upon us.

As participants, many of us look forward to the change in seasons. Living in the Midwest, I enjoy the four seasons and almost set my clock by the arrival of certain perennials and birds in the spring, the fireflies in the summer, the sound of crickets chirping in the fall, and the first snowfall in early winter. These are things we anticipate because they remind us of the normalcy and expectancy of change in the seasons.

All change, however, is not welcomed. A death in the family, a missing pet, a move out of state, or a loss of a friend or mentor, can cause changes that are dreaded rather than anticipated. But change is inevitable and needs to be understood as an opportunity for growth and development. Stagnant feelings and surroundings do little to nurture our spirits. Change by its nature causes us to step outside our comfort zone and spiritually stretch to new heights.

So, change can bring hope or hurt initially; but in the process of change, beneficial growth can occur. When change impacts you, why not ask yourself what this process now frees you up to do. What gifts are hidden in the change? How can you embrace it and grow beyond your own limitations? These are the diamonds in the rough that can be mined for your future benefit. Prospect in your own backyard and uncover these gems. They just might be priceless.

Eternal Change

Dr. Napoleon Hill

Strange also is the fact that only one thing is permanent in this universe—eternal change. Nothing remains exactly the same for even a second. Even the physical body in which we live changes completely with astonishing rapidity.

You can test these statements against your own experience.

When a person is struggling for recognition and to get a few dollars ahead, seldom will he find anyone to give him a needed lift. But once he makes the grade—and no longer needs help—people stand in line to offer him aid.

Through what I call the law of attraction, like attracts like in all circumstances. Success attracts greater success. Failure attracts more failure.

Throughout our lives we are the beneficiaries or victims of a swiftly flowing stream which carries us onward toward either success or failure.

The idea is to get on the "success beam" rather than on the "failure beam."

How can you do this? Simple. The answer lies in adopting a positive mental attitude that will help you shape the course of your own destiny rather than drifting along at the mercy of life's adversities.

Source: *Miami Daily News,* Summer 1956.

Chapter 42

LIFE'S DRIFTERS AND NON-DRIFTERS

For many, we have a defined routine to our daily lives. We know that we must wake up at a specific time, go to work, take care of the family and ourselves. Most of us are cognizant of the benefits to eating healthy, exercising, relaxing and spending time with others. But to what extent are we prepared for the "out of the ordinary" situations?

—AMY ATCHA

By deciding to become a non-drifter in life, you not only make life easier for yourself but for others. If you have to constantly be reminded about your obligations, your appointments, and your daily tasks, aren't you abdicating the life you were given? Strength of character involves personal initiative, discipline, and persistence. Each of these characteristics gives us an increasingly stronger foothold on life. By creating our own habits of thought and sticking to them, we tell our ego who really is in charge.

Positive actions that are repeated daily contribute to our character makeup. People know us by our deeds, not our talk.

While it's true that what you think about you bring about, the missing step in the sequence is action. W. Clement Stone knew this for a fact and his command, "Do it now!" is what put him over the top. By doing it now, we enforce our determination to succeed because we tell our "critic" that we refuse to be deterred by the fear of criticism. The simple phrase, "Do it now!" jump-starts our success because of the action it causes us to take.

Movement is the necessary key. Without it, there would be no foundation underneath our dreams.

So, decide today to do what it is you need to do, and then begin the process as Dr. Hill states, "whether you are ready or not." The psychology behind beginning now is a great motivator since it conditions us for future actions. Begin to put one foot literally in front of the next as you begin your success journey. You already have an idea of what actions need to be taken, so begin today to do the things that a non-drifter does. These will accumulate in short order and soon you will be in the higher brackets of those who do not drift.

Habits of Thought

Dr. Napoleon Hill

Drifters make no attempt to discipline or control their thoughts and never learns the difference between positive thinking and negative thinking. Drifters in life allow their minds to drift with any stray thought which may float into it. People who drift in connection with their thought habits are sure to drift on other subjects as well.

In an allegorical account of an interview with the devil, it was stated that the devil said he feared nothing except that the world might sometime produce a thinker who would use his own mind, adding significantly that he controlled all drifters who neglected to use their own minds. The devil is not the only one who exploits the drifter. And drifters are the victims not only of all those who wish to exploit them, but they are also the victims of all the stray, negative thoughts which park themselves in their minds.

Non-drifters take full possession of their own minds through self-discipline and organizes definite plans and purposes. They direct their minds to whatever ends they desire keep their minds occupied with the things they want and off the things they do not want.

A positive mental attitude is the first and the most import-ant of the twelve riches of life, and it cannot be attained by the drifter. It can be attained only by a scrupulous regard for time, through habits of self-discipline.

No amount of time devoted to one's occupation can com-pensate for the benefits of a positive mental attitude, for this is the power which makes the use of time effective and productive.

A positive mental attitude does not grow voluntarily, like the weeds of the fields. It requires cultivation, through carefully disciplined habits of thoughts. And the greatest of all training grounds for the cultivation of a positive mental attitude is provided by our chosen occupation, where we spend the greatest part of our lives.

Here you may combine your efforts to make them financially productive and to develop a positive mental attitude. When you get your own thought habits under control, you will have yourself under control, but you cannot do it by drifting. Organize your thoughts. Decide what you want, to what position in life you aspire. Then plan ways and means to express your thoughts, in terms of organized action. Follow through with applied faith and unremitting persistence. This is the means by which you can become the master of your fate, the captain of your soul.

Waste no time worrying about what others may think. The important thing is what you think and do.

Source: Adapted from *PMA: Science of Success,* Educational Edition, Napoleon Hill Foundation, 1983; pages 463-464.

Chapter 43

CHOOSING A PACEMAKER

Napoleon Hill wrote that success in marriage required a common cause with sufficient harmony to subordinate selfishness. He was right of course, but he left out one essential ingredient—the willingness to endure.

—DR. J. B. HILL

Who are the heroes who inspire you? Who do you emulate or want to be like? Who are you interested in now, and in whom were you interested in the past? With which ancestors do you feel a close kinship? Jot down a list of ten individuals who guide your life. Select from your family, your culture, your nation, and your spiritual belief system. Now, ask yourself why these people are significant mentors for you, whether living or dead. As you begin to assess the reasons you relate to them, you will begin to excavate the beliefs, values, attitudes, interests, ideas, and thoughts that propel you forward in life.

Now that you have identified your pacemakers, consider whether you are learning all you can learn from each of them. By knowing who you admire and what they are accomplishing or have accomplished in their lives, you begin to set a route for the journey you too are undertaking. Remember, if you want to arrive at your destination, you must first have one in mind. Otherwise, one destination is as good as the next. Just as a youngster plays "grownup" by stepping into Daddy's or Mommy's shoes that are too large for his or her little feet to fill, you too have to find some big shoes to fill before you can step toward success!

Take a moment now to identify current individuals whom you want to label as pacemakers in your life. Watch them closely, and then follow their lead. Hopefully, you will not only catch up to them, but surpass them in the race to your finish line. By aspiring to greatness, you hitch your wagon to that specific star in the galaxy that has your name on it! Make certain that you reach that star and register it in your name before someone else beats you to it.

Choose a Pacemaker

Dr. Napoleon Hill

Choose as your pacemaker some prosperous, self-reliant person who is obviously successful. Make up your mind not only to catch up with that person, but to excel; but do this silently, without mentioning to anyone what you're doing.

A number of years ago, while teaching a class down in Long Beach, California, the value of a pacemaker was brought out in a very vivid lesson. It was one of those terrifically foggy nights when you could not tell where you were except in relation to the white lines painted on the highway. The lights of the car did not penetrate very far and one had to creep along. A car was found that was equipped with fog lights and two high candlepower spotlights which could light up the white lines for a considerable distance. This extra lighting enabled the pacemaker to travel at near normal speed. We took advantage of his trail breaking and drove along behind him. It was evident that if he encountered any obstacles, he would give sufficient warning so that we could stop and avoid trouble.

So it is in life. If you pick out someone who is traveling the same road you have chosen, that person will light up the pitfalls for you, and thereby you may avoid some of them. Remember to carry your share of the load, however; and when you have passed your first pacemaker, assume the role for someone else.

When you select a pacemaker, be sure to choose one who keeps moving at the same speed, or faster, than you yourself wish to travel. If the person slows down too much, or turns off on a side road, you had better switch to another trailblazer.

Source: Adapted from *PMA: Science of Success,* Educational Edition, Napoleon Hill Foundation, 1983; page 115.

Chapter 44

POSITIVE SELF-TALK

Throughout America's history, some prominent leaders created rules for personal achievement or productive living. People expect and appreciate helpful rules from respected leaders. These rules derive from the unique perspectives, observations, or experiences of their authors. These rules were also used to further build the image, fame, or name recognition of every leader providing the rules.

—FORREST WALLACE CATO

Have you even been told any of the following? These pronouncements can serve like prophecies when spoken to children, individuals with low self-esteem, or just about anyone having a bad day.

1. You never do anything right!
2. There must be something wrong with you.
3. You got what you deserved.
4. You only care about yourself.
5. You're just lazy.
6. You must be stupid.

7. All you do is cause trouble.

8. You just think you're so special!

9. You'll never amount to anything.

10. You haven't heard anything I've been telling you.

Although seemingly well-intentioned, these negative statements that are supposed to cause a person to sit up, take notice, and improve—do the very opposite. When heard, these statements are transformed into self-talk that go something like this:

1. I never do anything right.

2. There's something wrong with me.

3. I deserve what I get.

4. I only care about myself.

5. I'm lazy.

6. I'm stupid.

7. I always cause trouble.

8. I'm nothing special.

9. I'll never amount to anything.

10. I never listen to anyone's advice.

Wow, as if by magic these "well-meaning" statements become negative affirmations that condition people to fail, because it is what they are programming their subconscious minds to bring about through repetition. Acknowledging this tendency in people to internalize negative commentary, it would be good practice and an antidote to the poisonous remarks if people learned to hear positive self-talk instead. By turning negatives into positives we can turn base metal into gold. This is the real alchemy of success. You can practice being an alchemist now by turning the above ten statements into nuggets of gold. I'll get you started: "I never do anything right," transmutes into, "I do everything right!" Say these two sentences out loud. Which one feels more magical?

Now, finish the rest.

Auto-Suggestion

Dr. Napoleon Hill

Émile Coué, the French psychologist, gave the world a very simple but practical formula for the maintenance of a health consciousness in one sentence. *Every day in every respect, I am getting better and better.* He recommended that this sentence be repeated many times daily, until the subconscious section of the mind picked it up, accepted it and began to carry it out to its logical conclusion in the form of good health.

The wise ones smiled not too tolerantly, when they heard of the Coué formula. But many people accepted it in good faith, put it to work in earnest, and discovered that it produced marvelous results, for it started them on the road toward the development of a health consciousness.

Another term for this is auto-suggestion. There are many articles about it and many convincing stories to be told on the subject. Seek them out if you feel the need of their support. Let me add one point. Do you recall that the subconscious mind can do only what the conscious mind believes? Belief is the most important ingredient in the functioning of the subconscious mind.

Thus a word of warning: one moment's doubt will destroy and paralyze the function of the subconscious mind. It is imperative that we remove all doubt, for it is like a door and it slams shut instantly on the idea you were developing in your subconscious mind. This explains the failures of those who laughed at Émile Coué, and all the doubters down through the endless progress of civilization. Edison, Marconi, and the Wright brothers didn't doubt. The doubters do not contribute to civilization.

Source: *PMA: Science of Success,* Educational Edition, Napoleon Hill Foundation, 1983; page 431.

Chapter 45

YOUR "OTHER SELF"

I think that people often make a mistake in a way that they think and talk about things a lot, but there is no action in order to translate those thoughts into riches. Thinking alone is nothing. Thinking and acting upon those thoughts is everything you need.

—MILOS BULATOVIC

Thanksgiving is an opportunity for us to express our gratitude for each other and for all the good things that have occurred in our lives throughout the year. All the good things life has to offer come in abundance when we first notice them and next send a "thank you" message back to the Universe for all the goodness that is gifted to us daily. This form of acknowledging and blessing what we like and enjoy causes us to pay attention and thereby receive more of the same.

Whenever we place our attention on something we magnify it. Just as a magnifying glass increases the size of what we are observing, so too the placement of our attention on something causes us to experience more of it in our lives.

Have you ever stayed away from stores for a while and then returned to them? Aren't you amazed at all the new things you see? Have you been on a long trip and then returned home to experience the joy of being in your own space? Things look different, don't they? It is good to go and good to return home. Life is cyclic. Just by noticing the good things in life, we can improve our attitude—and a good attitude improves our outcome.

Think of the little things in life that make a big difference. In the fall, I love the rustle of leaves, the colorful landscape, the smell of ripe produce, the feel of my cats' winter coats, the taste of pumpkin pie, and on and on. What would life be like without the enjoyment of little things? Big events are only every so often, but little joys are like the invisible faeries (sometimes called the little people) of the world—under every leaf and waiting in every nook and cranny. But angels, they only come around every so often. Don't wait for the archangels to appear in all their glory; look for the little people hidden in everyday events.

The message: Enjoy the here and now—know that today will be yesterday tomorrow, so do it now!

Unseen Guides

Dr. Napoleon Hill

Every individual is born with an accompanying group of un-seen Guides sufficient to supply all his or her needs; and with these Guides come definite penalties for neglect to recognize and use them, also definite rewards for their recognition and use. In the main, the rewards consist of the necessary wisdom to ensure the individual's success in carrying out his or her mission in life, whatever that may be, and to show the way to the most priceless of all riches—peace of mind.

Throughout this volume I have described, through many phrases and illustrations, the Supreme Secret of all human achievements. Those who discover this secret will receive with it the means of recognizing and bringing into their service the unseen Guides which may now lie dormant, awaiting recognition and the call to service.

The presence of these Guides, and evidence of their active service in one's behalf, will be recognized by the improvements and benefits which will begin to manifest themselves from the very day the Guides receive recognition and are given definite instructions.

Fantastic and impractical, does someone exclaim?

No, "miraculous" is a better word, because no one, so far as I know, has yet explained the source of these unseen Guides, or how or why they are assigned to guide the lives of every living person. But there are thousands of people among the students of the Science of Success who know that the Guides exist because they too have learned the method—the Supreme Secret—by which this guidance can be acquired.

The unseen Guides are housed in that "other self" which every person possesses; that self which one does not see when looking into a mirror; that self which does not recognize the word "impossible," nor the limitations of any nature whatsoever; that self which is the master of all physical pain, all sorrow, defeat, and temporary failure. Somewhere along the way, as you read this volume, your "other self" may jump out from behind the lines, where you can recognize it, if you have not already done so. When that point has been reached, turn down the page and mark it for future reference, for you will have come to a profound turning point of your life.

Nowhere in these remarks am I endeavoring to prove anything! I am only endeavoring to introduce the reader to that "other self" who, once it has been recognized, will provide all the proof anyone could desire. Which is only another way of saying I am trying to induce readers to look "within" for the answer to the riddle of life—to THINK for themselves!

Source: *You Can Work Your Own Miracles* by Napoleon Hill, Random House, NY, 1971; pages 48-49.

Chapter 46

TEN COMMANDMENTS
OF SUCCESS

*It is sad to realize that in the world we live in today,
if you do what you say you're going to do, in a reliable
and dependable fashion, it becomes noteworthy, and
you become legendary among your customers or circle
of influence.*

—JIM STOVALL

Have you ever felt that you have reached the end of your wits? Like giving up? Ready to throw in the towel? Unsure of where your next path will lead? Depressed because even though you have tried your hardest, you still are fighting an uphill battle? If you have answered "yes" to any of these questions, welcome to the world.

Knowing that there is a pit in every cherry, bones in the Lake Perch, and husks on the sweet corn doesn't stop us from making a delicious dinner from the ingredients. Likewise, the sidebars, detours, and hassles in life should not deter us from becoming the success we were born to be. Sidestepping the potholes and enduring the turbulence will bring us to our destination more quickly if we accept the fact that all going is not smooth. Sailing through life problem-free does not enhance the journey. Think of those who are fortunate and can supposedly cast their cares aside. Although from the outside looking in, their lives seem rich beyond compare, usually the veneer falls away when they are truly tested. The old saying that the grass is always greener on the other side of the fence is nothing more than a matter of perspective.

By gaining perspective on our lives, we can focus on what truly matters and ignore the rest. All battles need not be fought, nor every concern of the day addressed. By focusing on our passion in life, the sidebars can be intentionally overlooked and more progress made.

In Dr. Hill's Philosophy of Personal Achievement, he authored the Ten Commandments of Success. Read through the commandments daily and this will ensure that you are acquainting yourself with the basic success principles. If you use this list as a guide, you will begin to rise to any height of success to which you aspire as long as you do not violate the rights of another human being.

Philosophy of Personal Achievement

Dr. Napoleon Hill

1. Set your head and heart upon a DEFINITE MAJOR PURPOSE and go to work, right where you stand, to attain it; and begin NOW.

2. Adopt and follow the habit of GOING THE EXTRA MILE by rendering more service and better service than you are paid for, thus enlarging the space you may occupy in the world.

3. Control your MENTAL ATTITUDE and keep it always positive and free from the spirit of defeatism.

4. Apply the GOLDEN RULE in all your human relationships, no matter what others may do.

5. Learn all that others have discovered in connection with your occupation, job, or business, and profit by their experience, thus saving yourself both grief and loss of time.

6. Eat sparingly, of the right combination of foods, and make sure that your "system" is always free from toxic poisoning.

7. Keep your dominating thoughts upon the things you desire and demand of life, and off the things you do not desire.

8. Learn to transmute your sex emotion into the attainment of your DEFINITE MAJOR PURPOSE, at will, remembering that this is a creative force of unknown, unlimited possibilities.

9. If you work for another person, do your work THE BOSS'S WAY, not yours, and do it in a gracious, pleasing manner.

10. Instead of criticizing others (no matter how much they may deserve it) devote your time to the discovery of traits of your own which should be corrected lest they provide the basis of just criticism against you.

If followed, in a spirit of sincerity, these ten rules will help you to occupy all the space in the world which your talents, education, and experience entitle you to enjoy, and they will bring you that sort of peace of mind which surpasses understanding.

Source: *Law of Success* by Napoleon Hill.

Chapter 47

THE VALUE OF A SOUND CHARACTER

Occasionally we must endure personal setbacks until
we wrest victory from the jaws of temporary defeat.
We must dedicate ourselves to the goal of our choosing
and pursue that goal until victory is ours with the
Faith that in our time of greatest peril or adversity
Providence will come to our aid.

—ELIEZER ALPERSTEIN

As time passes, the more faith I put into Providence. This faith in something or somebody beyond our current understanding requires that we submit to a divine will or plan. This does not mean that our lives are preordained and set in lock-step fashion beginning to end, but rather that sometimes we do not understand something fully enough to see beyond the here and now, or in other words, we do not see the big picture.

I have a friend who struggled greatly when she was dismissed from law school in Ohio because her first year grades were just a fraction too low to advance to the second year of study. She was on a donor's scholarship and try as she might, she had to give it up because she had to meet a certain grade point average set by the school. She was one-tenth of a percentage point too low! This person already had a bachelor's degree, a master's degree, and a degree in canon law. She had been a teacher, a school principal, and is a Sister of Providence. I watched her question again and again why this happened as she was trying to begin a new chapter in her life; but as she did so, she also reminded herself that she believed in Providence, in fact she was a Sister of Providence, so she had to accept this "failure" as divine will.

When she accepted this change of course in her life, she moved on to a different state and began a new assignment. Within an amazingly short period of time she advanced to the second-in-command of a huge diocese. She was in her sixties when all this began to take place and she served for more than ten years. If asked her how she felt about Providence, and I am certain she would say that a bend in the road is not the end of the road. Somehow, because she accepted the "no" from the law school, she found her true position in life. Did Providence guide her? I believe, as she indicated to me, that yes she was directed to this choice because doors were closed and she had to open a new one.

So I have learned a great lesson from my friend. When doors close on you, it is always because Providence has a grander destination in mind for you than the one you would have chosen for yourself. Faith is the opposite of fear. Let that door close, and advance toward the one you least expect will lead you to your dream. Believe and you will succeed.

Your Hope of Success

Dr. Napoleon Hill

If you accept defeat as an inspiration to try again, with renewed confidence and determination, the attainment of your success will be only a matter of time. If you accept defeat as final and allow it to destroy your confidence, you may as well abandon your hope of success.

Every defeat you meet will mark an important turning point in your life, for defeat will bring you face to face with the necessity of renewing confidence in yourself, or of admitting that confidence is lacking.

Defeat often serves to relieve a person of conceit. But there is a difference between conceit and self-reliance based upon an honest inventory of one's character. People who quit when defeat overtakes them thereby indicate that they mistook their conceit for self-reliance.

If people have genuine self-reliance, they also have sound character, for one springs from the other. And a sound character does not yield to defeat without a fight.

Source: Adapted from *PMA: Science of Success,* Educational Edition, Napoleon Hill Foundation, 1983; page 395.

Chapter 48

SELF-CONFIDENCE FORMULA

After my first visit to the campus, I could not turn down a chance to attend University of Virginia College at Wise. The campus was beautiful; the staff was very polite; and I felt an instant bond with my teammates. The campus provided a sense of comfort even with my great distance from home.

—AMBER CARTER, GRADUATING SENIOR

In aspiring toward success, one characteristic a person must possess is self-confidence. This ability to be self-assured and ready to undertake any challenge is a gift that parents give to children at an early age. This "You can do it" attitude enables youngsters to believe in themselves and their abilities strongly enough to begin and to finish a task. Parents who praise, encourage, and enable a child to do something successful are laying the cornerstones for a lifetime of success.

Believing in yourself because of your accomplishments is one way to pat yourself on the back when parents are not around to do it. Another way is to recite Napoleon Hill's self-confidence formula daily. This formula serves as a positive reminder that we are responsible for charting our own course to success.

An additional way is to memorize the poem, "It Couldn't Be Done," by Edgar A. Guest. Many speakers recite this during their presentations and this creates a dynamic presentation piece and also causes the audience to respond warmly. Try reciting it, and notice how enthusiasm grows inside you and awakens your spirit of success.

Self-Confidence Formula

Dr. Napoleon Hill

1. I know that I have the ability to achieve the object of my definite purpose in life; therefore, I demand of myself persistent, continuous action toward its attainment, and I here and now promise to render such action.

2. I realize the dominating thoughts of my mind will eventually reproduce themselves in outward, physical action, and gradually transform themselves into physical reality; therefore, I will concentrate my thoughts for thirty minutes daily, upon the task of thinking of the person I intend to become, thereby creating in my mind a clear mental picture.

3. I know through the principle of auto-suggestion, any desire that I persistently hold in my mind will eventually seek expression through some practical means of attaining the object back of it; therefore, I will devote ten minutes daily to demanding of myself the development of self-confidence.

4. I have clearly written down a description of my definite chief aim in life, and I will never stop trying, until I shall have developed sufficient self-confidence for its attainment.

5. I fully realize that no wealth or position can long endure, unless built upon truth and justice; therefore, I will engage in no transaction which does not benefit all whom it affects. I will succeed by attracting to myself the forces I wish to

use, and the cooperation of other people. I will induce others to serve me, because of my willingness to serve others. I will eliminate hatred, envy, jealousy, selfishness, and cynicism, by developing love for all humanity, because I know that a negative attitude toward others can never bring me success. I will cause others to believe in me, because I will believe in them, and in myself. I will sign my name to this formula, commit it to memory, and repeat it aloud once a day, with full faith that it will gradually influence my thoughts and actions so that I will become a self-reliant and successful person.

Source: *Think and Grow Rich* by Napoleon Hill, Chapter 3, Faith.

It Couldn't Be Done

by Edgar A. Guest

Somebody said that it couldn't be done,
But he with a chuckle replied
That "maybe it couldn't," but he would be one
Who wouldn't say so till he'd tried.
So he buckled right in with the trace of a grin
on his face. If he worried he hid it.
He started to sing as he tackled the thing
That couldn't be done, and he did it.
Somebody scoffed: "Oh, you'll never do that;
At least no one ever has done it";
But he took off his coat and he took off his hat,
And the first thing we knew he'd begun it.
With a lift of his chin and a bit of a grin,
Without any doubting or quiddit,
He started to sing as he tackled the thing
That couldn't be done, and he did it.
There are thousands to tell you it cannot be done,
There are thousands to prophesy failure;
There are thousands to point out to you one by one,
The dangers that wait to assail you.
But just buckle in with a bit of a grin,
Just take off your coat and go to it;
Just start to sing as you tackle the thing
That "cannot be done," and you'll do it.

Chapter 49

YOUR TRUE CALLING

Our financial economy does need a boost so buying and giving materials things to children is the nature of our world (and yes, I'll still deliver the things on Christmas Eve). But our moral economy needs a much greater boost and there is no better way to turn that around than by giving love and time to children. Just love and time—it costs you nothing and gives so much.

—SANTA CLAUS

Finding our true calling in life is usually not an easy task. Many of us try on different hats as we experiment with our life's vocation, or personal calling. Sometimes, we begin to close in on what gives our life true purpose only to back away when we become frightened or concerned that we are unable to make a living at what we like to do. What we like to do or enjoy doing is usually what we are good at, and herein is our buried treasure: our calling or life's work.

It does not benefit someone to pursue a career in an area that only provides them financial security without personal satisfaction. Better to pursue a career that is short on finances but long on personal satisfaction. If you feel drawn to what you are doing, would do it for no monetary compensation whatsoever, are not compelled to watch the clock while you are doing it, and it harms no other living person, then you have found your calling or your talent.

Hidden assets are traits that are sometimes buried within and do not surface until a very real need calls them forth. It could be an adversity, a sense of dissatisfaction, or just the desire to do more that calls your greatest talents forward into your daily life. When these talents surface in your daily reality and are recognized by you, it is often like a homecoming because you have begun the journey within to your true self. Let these thoughts by Dr. Hill help you discover the wealth that is inside you—your personal treasure chest!

If we think about becoming ruthless, turning over our work to someone else because we are too lazy or distracted to do it, or fail to extend the proper courtesy to our co-worker, friend, loved one, or person on the street, the ultimate reflection is on us. On the other hand, if we extend the milk of human kindness to the person least likely to return the favor, do good for the sake of doing good and not for the sake of "What's in it for me," and be positive-minded because a positive attitude is the right mental attitude in all circumstances, then the Universe will pave the way for us to do the work we are most suited to do. We then work toward fulfilling our destiny when we keep an open channel instead of blocking the flow.

According to Dr. Hill, universal law never fails, and if the mantra "What you think about you become" is the pathway to success or failure, does it make any sense to focus on what we do not want in our lives? Always be good, do good, and you will have good. Good flows from good. Recognize this and you will be on the high road to success.

Using Your Hidden Assets

Dr. Napoleon Hill

Each of us has locked within us all that is necessary to achieve wealth and greatness. It's merely a matter of learning to use these hidden assets, of investing them so to speak, so we can cash in on them.

The tragic thing is that so many go through life without ever putting them to use. Sometimes, trouble and adversity is necessary to make people use their resourcefulness and brain power to achieve success.

A bookkeeper lost his job as Christmas was approaching. He had no money to buy his 10-year-old son a gift. Instead of merely despairing, he went to work making the boy a gift.

Using two wheels from a discarded baby carriage, a few pieces of lumber from the basement, and some bright red paint, he constructed a toy that captured the attention of the entire neighborhood.

Other children wanted similar toys. The demand grew so fast that the unemployed bookkeeper turned his basement into a factory, then moved his production to a real industrial plant.

The toy the bookkeeper designed was called the "scooter."

Or consider the case of a soldier returned from World War I. He had been a salesman before the war but was now unemployed. He used his hidden assets too. He took a chunk of ice cream, stuck a stick in it for a handle, dipped it in chocolate covering—and the Eskimo Pie was born!

Then there was a young man working as a filling station helper in Dallas. The work was hard, hours long, pay short—all adding up to a state of mind I call "constructive discontentment."

The young man began selling for a publisher of children's books. But instead of approaching parents, he made friends with school teachers and got their permission to tell the children in class about his books.

Then he would ask the children to arrange an appointment with their parents so he could sell them the books. The plan worked wonderfully and the last time I saw the young man he was preparing to go into the publishing business for himself.

Have you searched carefully for any "hidden" resources you've overlooked simply because they weren't in some form you could bank immediately?

Have you some plan or idea which might prove of great value if you brought it into the open and put it to use?

A very successful man once gave this splendid formula for gaining wealth.

"Get some useful item that will bring repeat sales," said he. "Then put everything you have into taking it to the millions of people who need it."

His name was F. W. Woolworth. He didn't create anything new. He merely took something old and gave it a new method of sales and distribution.

The opportunities our country offers today are greater than ever—and growing constantly. Think, for example, of the millions to be made by someone who devises some simple method of reducing traffic accidents.

Somewhere you have unused assets. Put them to work for you and make yourself financially independent.

Source: *Success Unlimited,* December 1966; pages 33-34.

Chapter 50

THE TIME HAS CO ME

Many people tend to live in either the past or future.
These are illusions and have no substance. The real
beauty of life lies mainly in the moment. When you
start to cherish your moments with gratitude for the
beauty of life and nature around you, life brings lots
of positive energy. You can use this energy to build
and create your dreams.

—MICHAEL TELAPARY

N ew Year's Eve is generally a time given over to recalling
what has transpired during the ending year. It is a
nostalgic time for reminiscing and reviewing all the experiences
that life has brought about in our day-to-day existence. It
is also a time for anticipating what changes we can make,
what cycles we can break, and what patterns we can undo in
order to document improvement in our lives. It is list-making
time and time to contractually put things on paper that we
choose to commit to in the coming year. A goal of furthering
education, dedicating more time to family, accomplishing
persistent unfulfilled dreams, righting wrongs, and just doing
what has been left undone for too long are all items on many
people's lists.

My goals never seem to change, but this year I am going to make my goals a priority. Too often they are relegated to the back burners of life, and I find myself resenting other goals that sneak in and jockey for a prime spot on my list. Usually these goals are not my own, but from someone else's agenda. The person making the request just needs this one thing done and promises that no more favors will be requested. Well, you know the rest of the story since this scenario plays out in all our lives.

Napoleon Hill talks about the law of compensation, and essentially this means that the good that you do will return to you with interest!

I believe this to be true, and have experienced it myself, but I want to remind you that we need to be good to ourselves too. Neglect of our personal dreams does not get us any bonus points. It only makes us resentful and hard to be around. So, prime your own pump first and then give to others from the overflow. This works because we honor who we are and acknowledge our personalized mission on this planet. If we fail to fulfill our birth contract, Napoleon Hill reminds us that we may just get the same assignment again the next time around! This is one way that we can rest assured that we are doing what we were put here to do for the good of humankind.

Clock of Time

Dr. Napoleon Hill

The hands of the Clock of Time are moving swiftly onward! We cry out, "Backward, turn backward, O Time in your flight," but Time does not heed your cries.

It is later than you think!

Arouse yourself, fellow wayfarer; awake and take possession of your own mind while you still have enough Time to become, during the yet unexpired future, that which you would have liked to have been in the past.

Make the most of your present allotment of Time, with the hope that you will not have to reincarnate in order to do the job all over again because of neglect.

You have been warned!

Now the responsibility is YOURS. There is a simple test by which you may judge whether or not you have been using your Time to best advantage. If you have attained peace of mind and material opulence sufficient for your needs, your Time has been properly used. If you have not attained these blessings, your Time has not been properly used, and you should begin now to search for the circumstances in connection with which you have fallen short.

The truly great people have no such reality as "idle time," because they keep their minds geared eternally to patterns of constructive thought. By this profound use of their Time, they develop an alert sixth sense through which they look, listen, and see from within.

If negative thoughts stray into the minds of the truly great, these thoughts are immediately transmuted into positive thoughts and exercised by positive physical action appropriate to their nature.

Tick, tick, tick—the pendulum of the Clock of Time is swinging rapidly!

The entire face of civilization is undergoing an uplifting operation.

Mr. Right and Mr. Wrong are engaged in mortal combat for supremacy. The Time has come for everyone to stand up and be counted. The use each of us makes of our individual allotment of Time will tell whose side each of us is on—Mr. Right's or Mr. Wrong's.

Something has speeded up the Clock of Time so rapidly that the last half of the twentieth century will reveal to humankind more individual opportunities for self-improvement than have been revealed during the entire past of humankind's existence.

Your share of these vast OPPORTUNITIES may be embraced and used only by the way you relate yourself to TIME!

Source: *You Can Work Your Own Miracles* by Napoleon Hill, Fawcett-Columbine, NY, 1971; pages 119-120.

"WHATEVER THE MIND CAN
CONCEIVE AND BELIEVE,
THE MIND CAN ACHIEVE."

For more information about Napoleon Hill and available products, please contact the following locations:

NAPOLEON HILL WORLD LEARNING CENTER
Purdue University Calumet
2300 173rd Street
Hammond, IN 46323-2094
Judith Williamson, Director
Uriel "Chino" Martinez, Assistant & Graphic Designer
Telephone: 219-989-3173 or 219-989-3166
Email: nhf@purduecal.edu

THE NAPOLEON HILL FOUNDATION
University of Virginia—Wise College Relations, Apt. C
1 College Avenue
Wise, VA 24293
Don Green, Executive Director
Annedia Sturgill, Executive Assistant
Telephone: 276-328-6700
Email: napoleonhill@uvawise.edu
Website: www.naphill.org